W9-BOL-937

Editor:	Maria Elvira Gallardo, MA
Cover Illustrator:	Karl Edwards
Designer/Production:	Rebekah O. Lewis
Cover Designer:	Barbara Peterson
Art Director:	Moonhee Pak
Project Director:	Betsy Morris, PhD

Table of Contents

Introduction

More I'm Through! What Can I Do? is a one-stop resource that addresses this all-too-familiar question teachers hear from students who finish early. The high-interest, ready-to-use puzzles, riddles, brainteasers, and mazes can be completed with minimal teacher assistance and help sharpen language arts, math, creative thinking, and critical thinking skills. This new series is a follow-up to our best-selling titles *I'm Through! What Can I Do?*

GETTING STARTED

Use any of the following suggestions to create a simple, structured environment that allows students to access these activities independently and keeps busy classrooms running smoothly.

1. Create individual student packets using all of the activity pages. Have students keep the packets in their desks and complete pages if they finish their assigned work early.

2. Create smaller packets by content areas (language arts and math) to use at centers. Store each set of packets in a file folder. Attach a class list to the outside of each folder. Have students cross out their names after they complete the packet.

3. Use activity pages individually as

   - supplements to specific lessons
   - homework assignments
   - substitute teacher's helpers
   - three-minute transition activities
   - morning warm-up or after-lunch refocusing activities

HELPFUL TIPS TO FREE YOUR TIME

   - Allow students to consult classmates to figure out puzzles.
   - Encourage students to correct each other's work.
   - Place copies of the answer key in an accessible area for students to pull as needed for self-correction.
   - Give students copies of the Student Recording Sheet (page 4) to keep track of completed activity pages. Have students color in or check off each activity after it is completed.

However you choose to use the activity pages, let *More I'm Through! What Can I Do?* assist you in establishing a constructive and productive classroom environment.

Name: _____

Keep track of your work by filling in the box after completing the activity.

p. 5	p. 6	p. 7	p. 8	p. 9	p. 10	p. 11	p. 12	p. 13	p. 14
p. 15	p. 16	p. 17	p. 18	p. 19	p. 20	p. 21	p. 22	p. 23	p. 24
p. 25	p. 26	p. 27	p. 28	p. 29	p. 30	p. 31	p. 32	p. 33	p. 34
p. 35	p. 36	p. 37	p. 38	p. 39	p. 40	p. 41	p. 42	p. 43	p. 44
p. 45	p. 46	p. 47	p. 48	p. 49	p. 50	p. 51	p. 52	p. 53	p. 54
p. 55	p. 56	p. 57	p. 58	p. 59	p. 60	p. 61	p. 62	p. 63	p. 64
p. 65	p. 66	p. 67	p. 68	p. 69	p. 70	p. 71	p. 72	p. 73	p. 74
p. 75	p. 76	p. 77	p. 78	p. 79	p. 80	p. 81	p. 82	p. 83	p. 84
p. 85	p. 86	p. 87	p. 88	p. 89	p. 90	p. 91			

More I'm Through! What Can I Do? Grade 3 © 2008 Creative Teaching Press

Name: _____   Date: _____

Magic Word Square #1

How many words can you find in the Magic Word square? Write the words you find on the lines below. There are more than 40 words!

Rules to remember:

- The words you find must have three or more letters.
- Start on any square and move one square at a time in any direction. You many not skip a square!
  Examples: **PAIN** is allowed because each square is touching another square.
      WAND is not allowed because the squares with the letters **N** and **D** are not touching each other.
- You may not use the same letter square twice in a row.
- Plurals are allowed.
- No proper nouns! (*Example:* Ana)

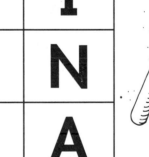

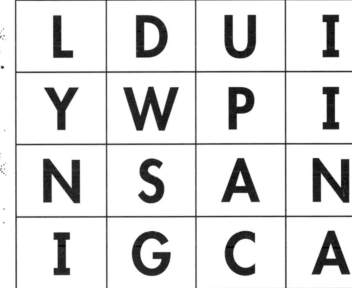

L	D	U	I
Y	W	P	I
N	S	A	N
I	G	C	A

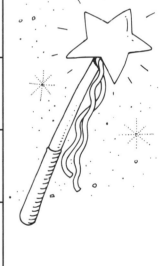

Words I Found

_____   _____   _____

_____   _____   _____

_____   _____   _____

_____   _____   _____

_____   _____   _____

Name: _____   Date: _____

Magic Word Square #2

How many words can you find in the Magic Word square? Write the words you find on the lines below. There are more than 65 words!

Rules to remember:

- The words you find must have three or more letters.
- Start on any square and move one square at a time in any direction. You many not skip a square!
  Examples: **LOAN** is allowed because each square is touching another square.
  OPEN is not allowed because the squares with the letters **E** and **N** are not touching each other.
- You may not use the same letter square twice in a row.
- Plurals are allowed.
- No proper nouns! (*Example*: Gena)

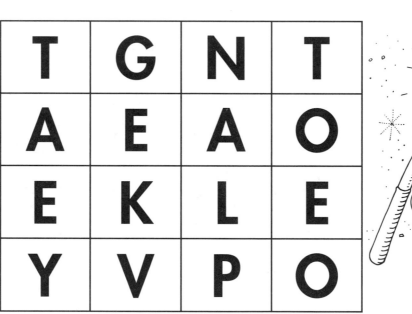

T	G	N	T
A	E	A	O
E	K	L	E
Y	V	P	O

Words I Found

_____ _____ _____

_____ _____ _____

_____ _____ _____

_____ _____ _____

_____ _____ _____

More I'm Through! What Can I Do? Grade 3 © 2008 Creative Teaching Press

Name: _____ Date: _____

Magic Word Square #3

How many words can you find in the Magic Word square? Write the words you find on the lines below. There are more than 95 words!

Rules to remember:

- The words you find must have three or more letters.
- Start on any square and move one square at a time in any direction. You many not skip a square!
- You may not use the same letter square twice in a row.
- Plurals are allowed.
- No proper nouns! (*Example*: Sam)
- The star can count for any letter!

S	L	M
I	★	V
P	H	E

Words I Found

_____ _____ _____

_____ _____ _____

_____ _____ _____

_____ _____ _____

_____ _____ _____

Magic Word Square #4

How many words can you find in the Magic Word square? Write the words you find on the lines below. There are more than 50 words!

Rules to remember:

- The words you find must have three or more letters.
- Start on any square and move one square at a time in any direction. You many not skip a square!
- You may not use the same letter square twice in a row.
- Plurals are allowed.
- No proper nouns! (*Example*: Zoe)
- The star can count for any letter!

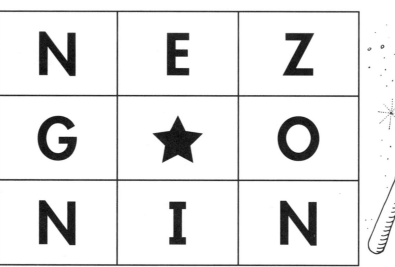

N	E	Z
G	★	O
N	I	N

Words I Found

_____   _____   _____

_____   _____   _____

_____   _____   _____

_____   _____   _____

_____   _____   _____

More I'm Through! What Can I Do? Grade 3 © 2008 Creative Teaching Press

Name: _____

Date: _____

Fun Words

For each category write a word that begins with the letter on the left. Score one point for each correct answer. Earn five bonus points for any category where you have no incorrect answers or blanks. Use books, encyclopedias, and other reference materials if you need help finding a word for any category.

Letter	Something Round	Form of Transportation	Song Title	A Game to Play	Something Made of Wood	Score
S						
P						
H						
W						
T						

Total	
Bonus	
Final Score	

Name: _____ Date: _____

Rhyming Word Robot

Use this code to color the robot:

rhymes with **bake** = red
rhymes with **beat** = yellow
rhymes with **bring** = green

rhymes with **best** = brown
rhymes with **bright** = orange
rhymes with **blot** = blue

rhymes with **bay** = purple
rhymes with **bit** = black

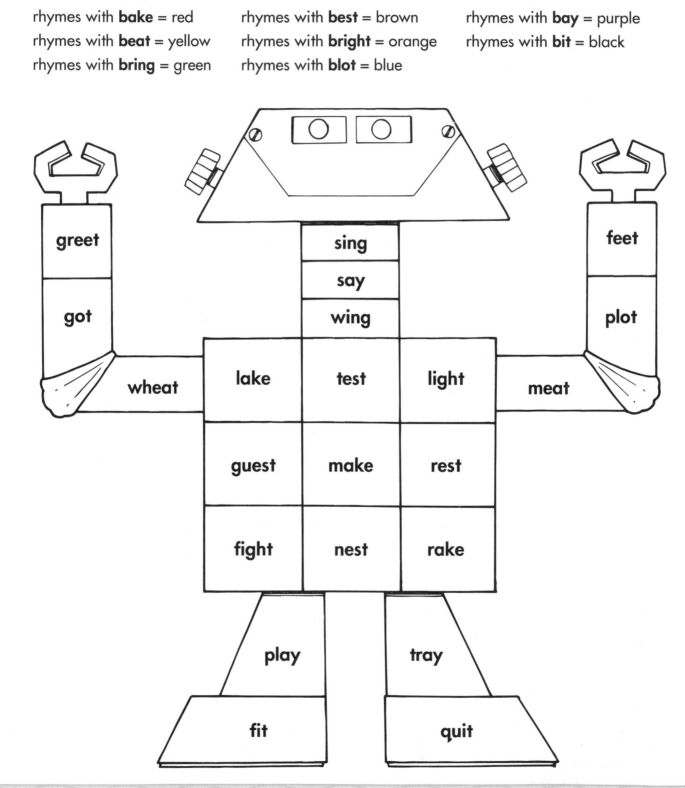

Mammals Word Scramble

Unscramble each of the mammal names below. Copy the letters in the numbered cells to the cells below with the same number in order to solve the riddle.

TIRGE ⬜⬜⬜⬜⬜
14

REQSULRI ⬜⬜⬜⬜⬜⬜⬜⬜
8

HAEMSRT ⬜⬜⬜⬜⬜⬜⬜
15 3

NUKKS ⬜⬜⬜⬜⬜
11

EBRAZ ⬜⬜⬜⬜⬜
4

NAADP ⬜⬜⬜⬜⬜
17 7

GOANAKRO ⬜⬜⬜⬜⬜⬜⬜⬜
9

LLAIROG ⬜⬜⬜⬜⬜⬜⬜
13

PAOLR BERA ⬜⬜⬜⬜⬜⬜ ⬜⬜⬜⬜
6

CONCAOR ⬜⬜⬜⬜⬜⬜⬜

GAFFIER ⬜⬜⬜⬜⬜⬜⬜
5

MELCA ⬜⬜⬜⬜⬜
16

NAPTELEH ⬜⬜⬜⬜⬜⬜⬜⬜
12 1

ROEHS ⬜⬜⬜⬜⬜
2

SEPHE ⬜⬜⬜⬜⬜
10

Why can't leopards play hide-and-seek?

⬜⬜⬜Y ⬜⬜⬜ ⬜W⬜Y⬜ ⬜⬜⬜⬜⬜⬜⬜
1 2 3   4 5 6   7 8 9 10   11 12 13 14 15 16 17

Name: _____   Date: _____

Outer Space Word Scramble

Unscramble each of the outer space words below. Copy the letters in the numbered cells to the cells below with the same number in order to solve the riddle.

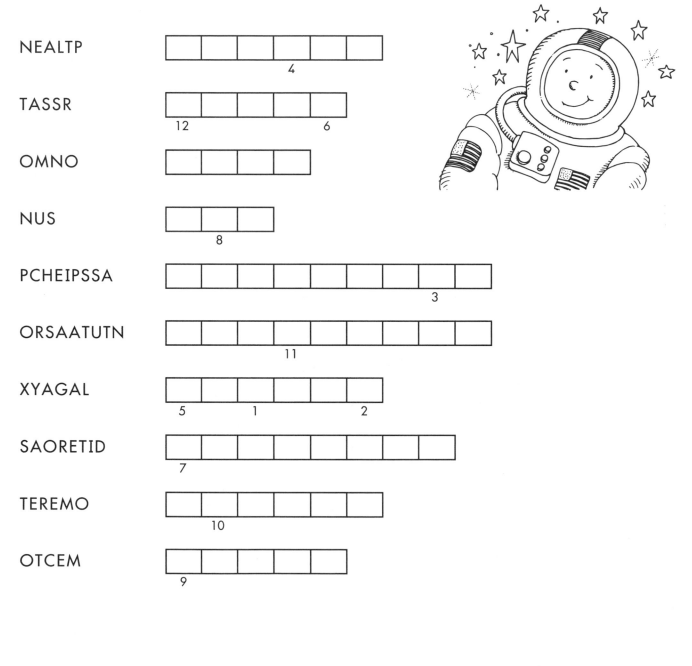

NEALTP   ☐ ☐ ☐ ☐ ☐ ☐
                     4

TASSR   ☐ ☐ ☐ ☐ ☐
           12   6

OMNO   ☐ ☐ ☐ ☐

NUS   ☐ ☐ ☐
              8

PCHEIPSSA ☐ ☐ ☐ ☐ ☐ ☐ ☐ ☐ ☐
                           3

ORSAATUTN ☐ ☐ ☐ ☐ ☐ ☐ ☐ ☐ ☐
              11

XYAGAL   ☐ ☐ ☐ ☐ ☐ ☐
           5   1   2

SAORETID   ☐ ☐ ☐ ☐ ☐ ☐ ☐ ☐
           7

TEREMO   ☐ ☐ ☐ ☐ ☐ ☐
              10

OTCEM   ☐ ☐ ☐ ☐ ☐
           9

On what do astronauts like to eat?

F	☐	☐	☐	☐		☐	☐	☐	☐	☐	☐	☐
	1	2	3	4	5	6	7	8	9	10	11	12

Around the House Word Scramble

Unscramble each of the words below. Copy the letters in the numbered cells to the cells below with the same number in order to solve the riddle.

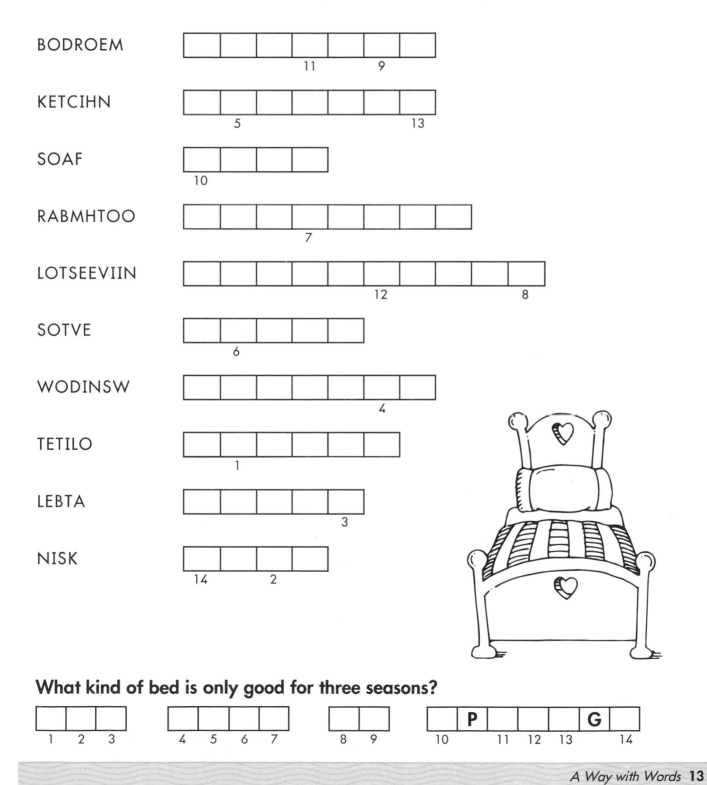

BODROEM

[ ][ ][ ][ ][ ][ ][ ]
        11   9

KETCIHN

[ ][ ][ ][ ][ ][ ][ ]
     5   13

SOAF

[ ][ ][ ][ ]
 10

RABMHTOO

[ ][ ][ ][ ][ ][ ][ ][ ]
       7

LOTSEEVIIN

[ ][ ][ ][ ][ ][ ][ ][ ][ ][ ]
            12   8

SOTVE

[ ][ ][ ][ ][ ]
     6

WODINSW

[ ][ ][ ][ ][ ][ ][ ]
              4

TETILO

[ ][ ][ ][ ][ ][ ]
 1

LEBTA

[ ][ ][ ][ ][ ]
           3

NISK

[ ][ ][ ][ ]
 14   2

What kind of bed is only good for three seasons?

[ ][ ][ ]   [ ][ ][ ][ ]   [ ][ ]   [ ][P][ ][ ][G][ ]
 1 2 3   4 5 6 7   8 9   10 11 12 13 14

Common Things

Look at each pair of items. Write at least three ways that they are similar and three ways they are different.

Similarities		Differences

More I'm Through! What Can I Do? Grade 3 © 2008 Creative Teaching Press

Draw the Noun

Read the word. Draw what the word names.

tent	mitt	doll
shutter	lock	nest
cake	bear	bean
sheep	soap	string

More I'm Through! What Can I Do? Grade 3 © 2008 Creative Teaching Press

Name: _____   Date: _____

Short *u* Words

Read the clues. Write the **short** *u* words.

you might need these if you break your leg cr_____	how you get squeaky clean scr_____
where you take a bath t_____	a kind of fruit pl_____
the name for a baby bear c_____	the opposite of **thin** pl_____
what everyone likes to have at a party f_____	the edge of a piece of bread cr_____
it shines high in the sky s_____	after breakfast and before dinner l_____
another word for **hop** j_____	you chew this g_____

Get Ahead

Circle all the words in the puzzle that have short vowel sounds. Did you find all 10?

```
H  X  R  L  S  B  O  N
A  Z  T  H  I  C  K  O
T  O  H  X  T  O  X  V
C  O  A  T  V  L  D  C
H  F  S  H  E  D  T  R
```

More I'm Through! What Can I Do? Grade 3 © 2008 Creative Teaching Press

Weather Word Search

Find and circle the weather words hidden in the puzzle. Words can be found going forward, backward, up, down, and diagonally.

blizzard	frost	lightning	temperature
cloud	hailstone	monsoon	thunder
cumulus	humidity	rain	tornado
cyclone	hurricane	sleet	typhoon
fog	icicle	snow	windstorm

F	R	O	S	T	E	E	L	S	I	H	U
T	Y	P	H	O	O	N	N	W	A	W	D
E	G	E	L	R	E	O	B	I	T	N	T
C	I	R	N	N	W	L	L	N	S	G	M
L	H	U	O	A	L	S	I	D	U	N	G
O	C	T	F	D	T	A	Z	S	L	I	E
U	R	A	C	O	R	Y	Z	T	U	N	L
D	O	R	N	Y	G	E	A	O	M	T	C
N	T	E	N	A	C	I	R	R	U	H	I
G	U	P	O	O	U	L	D	M	C	G	C
T	L	M	O	N	S	O	O	N	S	I	I
Y	R	E	D	N	U	H	T	N	O	L	A
G	Y	T	I	D	I	M	U	H	E	P	R

More I'm Through! What Can I Do? Grade 3 © 2008 Creative Teaching Press

Simple Machines Word Search

Find and circle the simple machine words hidden in the puzzle. Words can be found going forward, backward, up, down, and diagonally.

doorknob	inclined plane	pulley	seesaw
flagpole	knife	push	wagon
force	lever	ramp	wedge
fulcrum	nail	screw	wheel and axle
hammer	pull	screwdriver	zipper

Z	I	P	P	E	R	Y	B	C	Z	C	O	E	C	D
S	B	Z	S	R	K	B	M	F	B	U	N	M	Y	O
R	C	W	H	E	E	L	A	N	D	A	X	L	E	O
F	J	R	L	C	W	M	F	F	L	K	Y	V	L	R
F	O	I	E	A	K	L	M	P	S	N	H	P	L	K
K	A	R	S	W	A	N	D	A	Q	I	C	W	U	N
N	U	E	C	G	D	E	O	D	H	F	V	E	P	O
S	E	C	P	E	N	R	A	G	Q	E	J	H	I	B
S	E	O	P	I	L	U	I	L	A	P	U	L	L	Y
D	L	M	L	D	W	F	O	V	B	W	S	R	L	I
E	H	C	W	E	R	C	S	R	E	X	J	E	H	P
P	N	M	U	R	C	L	U	F	Q	R	V	G	F	A
I	U	Z	F	A	O	Z	M	U	X	E	B	D	U	K
U	M	S	Q	M	U	V	W	J	R	E	H	E	W	K
F	Z	T	H	P	H	K	C	I	R	T	R	W	J	Y

More I'm Through! What Can I Do? Grade 3 © 2008 Creative Teaching Press

Name: _____   Date: _____

Bodies of Water
and Landforms Word Search

Find and circle the bodies of water and landforms hidden in the puzzle. Words can be found going forward, backward, up, down, and diagonally.

bay	glacier	mountain	pond
canyon	gulf	ocean	river
coast	island	peninsula	sea
continent	lake	plain	stream
farmland	landform	plateau	valley

R	E	I	C	A	L	G	N	A	P	W	Q	E	D	O
U	E	M	K	T	H	D	L	I	C	F	J	N	U	C
T	S	A	O	C	N	U	X	S	A	A	A	D	D	E
U	J	C	C	O	S	A	K	A	F	L	N	J	O	A
L	A	F	P	N	Z	E	F	K	S	C	P	Y	U	N
N	A	E	I	C	O	N	T	I	N	E	N	T	O	I
H	U	N	T	C	Z	E	V	M	J	K	K	P	F	N
S	E	V	D	A	T	H	E	O	O	A	J	A	M	F
P	E	V	D	F	L	C	X	U	X	L	R	B	A	F
J	U	A	D	Y	O	P	Y	N	X	M	O	A	E	R
V	A	L	L	E	Y	R	G	T	L	Y	Z	Y	R	K
L	L	H	X	M	I	R	M	A	W	Y	O	D	T	T
G	U	L	F	V	Q	R	N	I	V	V	B	O	S	P
M	O	X	E	N	D	D	N	N	O	Z	O	E	K	P
S	A	R	A	N	W	Z	Z	D	S	P	E	V	X	G

Name: _____ Date: _____

Mixed Analogies Word Search

Fill in the missing word to compete each analogy. Then circle the words in the word search.
(**Hint**: The first letter of each word is provided for you.)

1. hot : cold : : l ___ ___ ___ : right

2. dark : n ___ ___ ___ ___ : : sunny : day

3. m ___ ___ ___ ___ : coins : : glass : windows

4. coffee : cup : : s ___ ___ ___ : bowl

5. hat : h ___ ___ ___ : : shoes : feet

6. bird : f ___ ___ ___ ___ : : snake : slithers

7. hair : p ___ ___ ___ ___ ___ : : fur : animals

8. stop : go : : r ___ ___ : green

9. boat : water : : p ___ ___ ___ ___ : air

10. city : c ___ ___ ___ ___ ___ : : state : country

11. cow : farm : : b ___ ___ ___ : forest

12. den : lion : : s ___ ___ : pig

G	T	E	N	I	C	I	D	E	M	C	X	B
R	A	E	B	R	V	E	L	P	O	E	P	W
S	P	H	U	R	K	S	W	O	O	D	R	S
Y	N	X	A	E	T	I	S	Y	P	K	I	O
T	F	P	B	D	U	F	L	E	F	T	Q	U
N	T	L	E	C	A	A	G	J	M	H	C	P
U	L	A	I	D	T	F	H	W	E	G	R	D
O	O	N	E	E	P	F	S	A	N	I	D	Y
C	I	E	M	E	S	M	D	G	H	N	K	T
M	O	T	A	D	P	O	L	E	B	Z	A	S

More I'm Through! What Can I Do? Grade 3 © 2008 Creative Teaching Press

Name: _____   Date: _____

Television Word Detective

How many words can you make using the letters in the word **television**? Write the words on the lines below. **Hint:** There are more than 100 words!

Rules:

- The words you make must have three or more letters.
- Your words can use letters in any order from **television**.
- You may only use each letter as many times as it appears in the word.
  Example: You may not list the word **test** because there is only one letter **t** in **television**.
- Plurals (e.g., **lines**) are allowed.
- No proper nouns (e.g., **Lee**) are allowed.

Scoring:

Three-letter word	= 1 point
Four-letter word	= 2 points
Five-letter word	= 3 points
Six-letter word	= 4 points
Word with seven or more letters	= 5 points

_____   _____   _____

_____   _____   _____

_____   _____   _____

_____   _____   _____

_____   _____   _____

_____   _____   _____

_____   _____   _____

_____   _____   _____

Number of words I found: _____   **Points:** _____

Communities Word Detective

How many words can you make using the letters in the word **communities**? Write the words on the lines below. **Hint:** There are more than 200 words!

Rules:

- The words you make must have three or more letters.
- Your words can use letters in any order from **communities**.
- You may only use each letter as many times as it appears in the word.
    Example: You may not list the word **common** because there is only one letter **o** in **communities**.
- Plurals (e.g., **items**) are allowed.
- No proper nouns (e.g., **Tim**) are allowed.

Scoring:

Three-letter word	= 1 point
Four-letter word	= 2 points
Five-letter word	= 3 points
Six-letter word	= 4 points
Word with seven or more letters	= 5 points

_____ _____ _____

_____ _____ _____

_____ _____ _____

_____ _____ _____

_____ _____ _____

_____ _____ _____

_____ _____ _____

Number of words I found: _____   **Points:** _____

More I'm Through! What Can I Do? Grade 3 © 2008 Creative Teaching Press

Name: _____   Date: _____

Solar System Word Detective

How many words can you make using the letters in the words **solar system**? Write the words on the lines below. **Hint:** There are more than 200 words!

Rules:

- The words you make must have three or more letters.
- Your words can use letters in any order from **solar** and **system**.
- You may only use each letter as many times as it appears in the two words.
    Example: You may not list the word **alarm** because there is only one letter **a** in the words **solar system**.
- Plurals (e.g., **arms**) are allowed.
- No proper nouns (e.g., **Sam**) are allowed.

Scoring:

Three-letter word	= 1 point
Four-letter word	= 2 points
Five-letter word	= 3 points
Six-letter word	= 4 points
Word with seven or more letters	= 5 points

_____   _____   _____

_____   _____   _____

_____   _____   _____

_____   _____   _____

_____   _____   _____

_____   _____   _____

_____   _____   _____

Number of words I found: _____   **Points:** _____

Family Similes

Complete each simile. Write an adjective in the first blank and a noun in the second blank of each sentence.

A mom is as _____

as a _____.

A dad is as _____

as a _____.

A brother is as _____

as a _____.

A sister is as _____

as a _____.

A dog is as _____

as a _____.

A cat is as _____

as a _____.

More I'm Through! What Can I Do? Grade 3 © 2008 Creative Teaching Press

Metaphor Medley

Answer each question by circling *Yes* or *No*. Then write what the metaphor means.

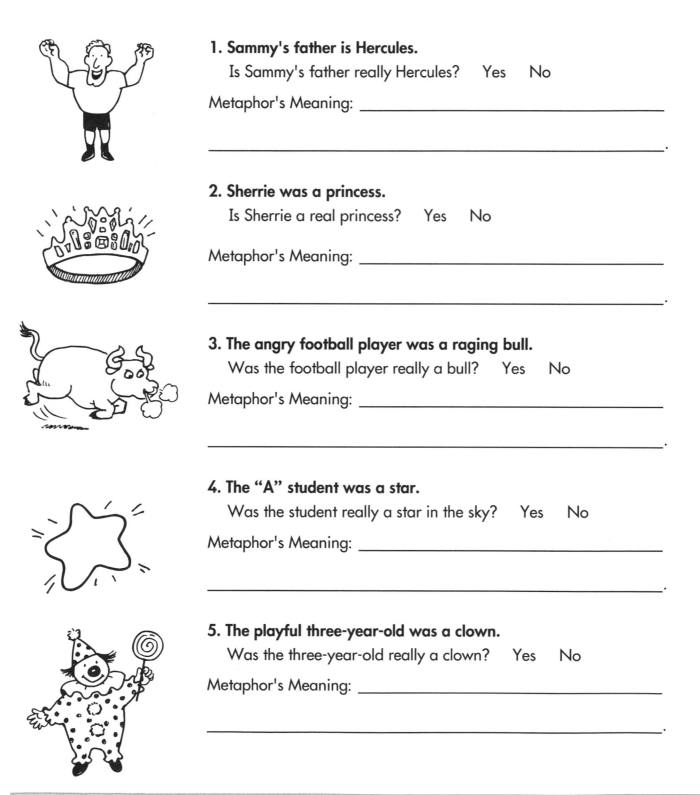

1. Sammy's father is Hercules.

Is Sammy's father really Hercules?   Yes   No

Metaphor's Meaning: _____

_____ .

2. Sherrie was a princess.

Is Sherrie a real princess?   Yes   No

Metaphor's Meaning: _____

_____ .

3. The angry football player was a raging bull.

Was the football player really a bull?   Yes   No

Metaphor's Meaning: _____

_____ .

4. The "A" student was a star.

Was the student really a star in the sky?   Yes   No

Metaphor's Meaning: _____

_____ .

5. The playful three-year-old was a clown.

Was the three-year-old really a clown?   Yes   No

Metaphor's Meaning: _____

_____ .

Word Blocks

Group A   **Group B**

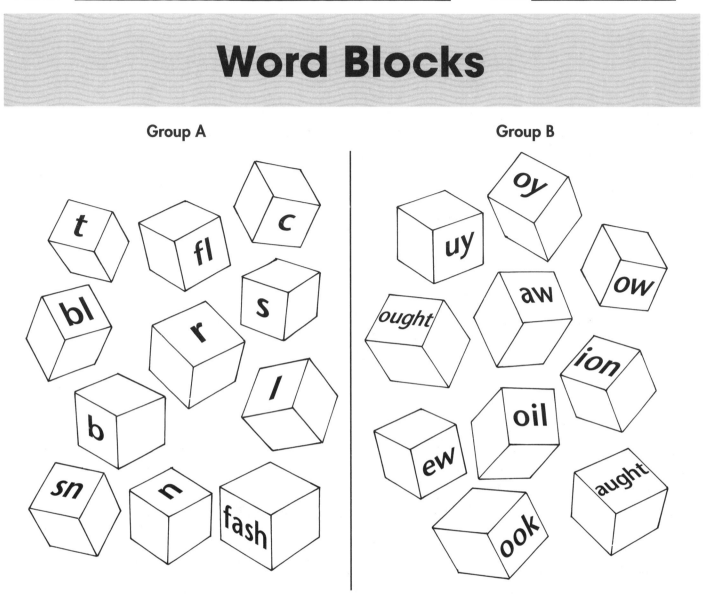

How many words can you make by combining pairs of the blocks together, one from each group?

_____ _____ _____

_____ _____ _____

_____ _____ _____

_____ _____ _____

_____ _____ _____

More I'm Through! What Can I Do? Grade 3 © 2008 Creative Teaching Press

Plurals Crossword Puzzle

A **noun** is the name of a person, place, or thing. A noun that is **singular** names only one person, place, or thing. A noun that is **plural** names more than one.

Write the plural form of each singular noun to complete the crossword puzzle. Put one letter in each box. The first one has been done for you.

Across
3. fox
5. baby
7. child
9. mouse
11. calf
13. goose
15. half
16. tomato

Down
1. woman
2. donkey
4. tool
6. bunny
8. hero
10. cargo
12. alto
14. man

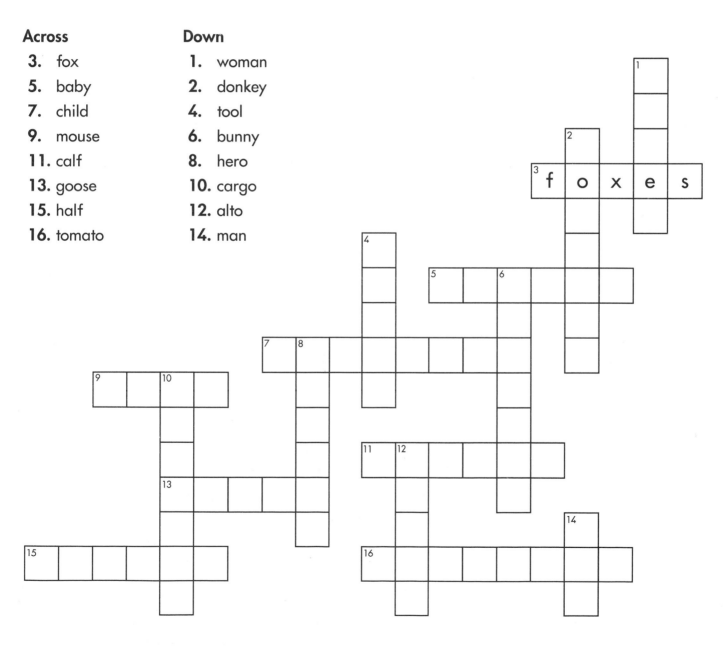

Name: _____ Date: _____

Five Senses Poem

Fill in the following lines to create a five senses poem describing a place. In the last line, name the place.

I see _____ .

I hear _____ .

I feel _____ .

I smell _____ .

I taste _____ .

Do you know where I am?

I am _____ .

More I'm Through! What Can I Do? Grade 3 © 2008 Creative Teaching Press

At School Word Links

Complete each school word by drawing a line between the word beginning on the left and the word ending that completes it on the right. Write the entire word on the line provided.

1. TE _____ •   • ICE

2. DE _____ •   • ESS

3. STU _____ •   • SER

4. RU _____ •   • YON

5. PEN _____ •   • ENCE

6. GL _____ •   • CIL

7. REC _____ •   • DENT

8. ERA _____ •   • SON

9. NOTE _____ •   • DER

10. BO _____ •   • BOOK

11. LES _____ •   • UTER

12. OFF _____ •   • SORS

13. SCIS _____ •   • SK

14. BIN _____ •   • ARD

15. SPEL _____ •   • WORK

16. COMP _____ •   • LING

17. CRA _____ •   • ST

18. ST _____ •   • LER

19. HOME _____ •   • UE

20. SCI _____ •   • UDY

More I'm Through! What Can I Do? Grade 3 © 2008 Creative Teaching Press

States Word Links

Complete the name of each state by drawing a line between the state name beginning on the left and the state name ending that completes it on the right. Write the complete name of the state on the line provided.

1. ALA _____ •
2. DELA _____ •
3. TE _____ •
4. OH _____ •
5. MARY _____ •
6. HA _____ •
7. VER _____ •
8. MONT _____ •
9. IO _____ •
10. ORE _____ •
11. ID _____ •
12. ARI _____ •
13. WASH _____ •
14. GEO _____ •
15. ALA _____ •
16. NEW _____ •
17. MISS _____ •
18. WYO _____ •
19. NEV _____ •
20. WISC _____ •

• LAND
• GON
• MONT
• ZONA
• ONSIN
• RGIA
• WARE
• WAII
• INGTON
• BAMA
• ISSIPPI
• MING
• ADA
• WA
• ANA
• IO
• XAS
• AHO
• YORK
• SKA

More I'm Through! What Can I Do? Grade 3 © 2008 Creative Teaching Press

Ship's Path to 50

Help the ship sail to its port. Begin at the number under "Start." Find the path through 14 numbers that add up to the **sum** of **50**. End at the number above "End." (Note: The path follows straight lines vertically and horizontally, not diagonally.) Write an addition sentence with the numbers you added together.

Start

3	2	3	4	5	6	7
6	2	4	0	3	2	1
9	3	6	4	0	1	2
4	5	2	1	5	6	7
3	2	4	3	9	9	8
4	7	6	7	2	1	4
9	7	5	1	4	3	0
2	1	3	2	3	4	2
4	3	6	3	9	7	5
7	2	4	4	0	5	9
2	4	1	0	6	0	8

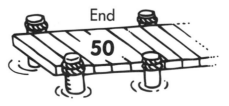

End

50

The number path I took to find the sum of 50 was:

_____ .

Ship's Path to 84

Help the ship sail to its port. Begin at the number under "Start." Find the path through 20 numbers that add up to the **sum** of **84**. End at the number above "End." (Note: The path follows straight lines vertically and horizontally, not diagonally.) Write an addition sentence with the numbers you added together.

Start

3	2	3	4	5	6	7
6	2	4	0	3	2	1
9	3	6	4	0	1	2
4	5	2	1	5	6	7
3	2	4	3	9	9	8
4	7	6	7	2	1	4
9	7	5	1	4	3	0
2	1	3	2	3	4	2
4	3	6	3	9	7	5
7	2	4	4	0	5	9
2	4	1	0	6	0	8

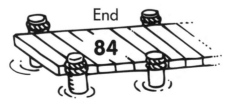

End

84

The number path I took to find the sum of 84 was:

_____ .

More I'm Through! What Can I Do? Grade 3 © 2008 Creative Teaching Press

Addition and Subtraction Riddle #1

Solve each equation. Then write the letter on the line for each answer. The letters will spell out the answer to the riddle.

1 K $10 = 4 + \underline{\quad}$

2 R $5 + \underline{\quad} = 20$

3 E $50 - \underline{\quad} = 42$

4 S $36 = 12 + \underline{\quad}$

5 C $15 + \underline{\quad} = 46$

6 C $18 - \underline{\quad} = 8$

7 A $\underline{\quad} + 9 = 23$

8 O $48 = 36 + \underline{\quad}$

9 A $22 - \underline{\quad} = 13$

10 D $15 + \underline{\quad} = 38$

11 F $19 + \underline{\quad} = 26$

12 D $\underline{\quad} - 30 = 11$

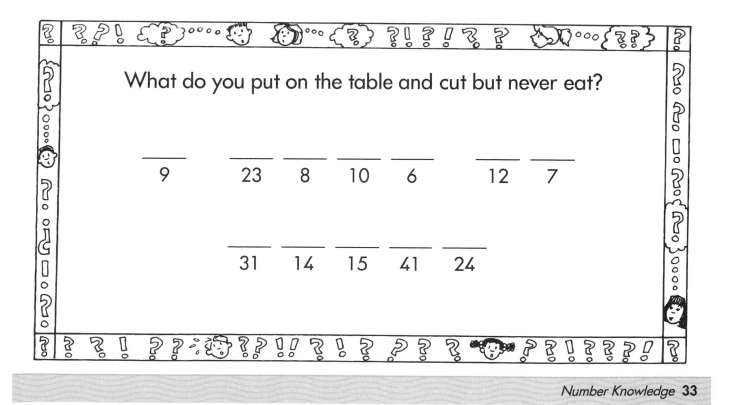

What do you put on the table and cut but never eat?

___ ___ ___ ___ ___   ___ ___
9   23   8   10   6   12   7

___ ___ ___ ___ ___
31   14   15   41   24

Addition and Subtraction Riddle #2

Solve each equation. Then write the letter on the line for each answer. The letters will spell out the answer to the riddle.

1 N $30 = 4 + \underline{\hspace{1cm}}$

2 R $15 + \underline{\hspace{1cm}} = 20$

3 E $50 - \underline{\hspace{1cm}} = 40$

4 B $36 = 15 + \underline{\hspace{1cm}}$

5 C $26 + \underline{\hspace{1cm}} = 46$

6 C $180 - \underline{\hspace{1cm}} = 80$

7 O $\underline{\hspace{1cm}} + 19 = 23$

8 O $48 = 26 + \underline{\hspace{1cm}}$

9 T $22 - \underline{\hspace{1cm}} = 15$

10 O $13 + \underline{\hspace{1cm}} = 38$

11 H $19 + \underline{\hspace{1cm}} = 32$

12 N $\underline{\hspace{1cm}} - 30 = 33$

For what vegetable do people throw away the outside, cook the inside, eat the outside, and then throw away the inside?

$\underline{\hspace{1cm}}$ $\underline{\hspace{1cm}}$ $\underline{\hspace{1cm}}$ $\underline{\hspace{1cm}}$ $\underline{\hspace{1cm}}$ $\underline{\hspace{1cm}}$
20   4   5   63   25   26

$\underline{\hspace{1cm}}$ $\underline{\hspace{1cm}}$ $\underline{\hspace{1cm}}$ $\underline{\hspace{1cm}}$ $\underline{\hspace{1cm}}$ $\underline{\hspace{1cm}}$
7   13   10   100   22   21

More I'm Through! What Can I Do? Grade 3 © 2008 Creative Teaching Press

Ice Cream Numbers

Using the three numbers on the ice cream cones, what is. . .

1. the smallest number you can make? _____

2. the largest number you can make? _____

3. the sum of the first and last numbers? _____

4. the number you get when you subtract
the second number from the last number? _____

5. the number you get when you multiply
the first and last numbers?

_____

6. the sum of the first two numbers? _____

7. the sum of the last two numbers? _____

8. the number you get when you subtract
the last number from the first number? _____

Clipboard Numbers

Using the three numbers on the clipboards, what is. . .

1. the smallest number you can make? _____

2. the largest number you can make? _____

3. the sum of the first and last numbers? _____

4. the number you get when you subtract
the second number from the last number? _____

5. the number you get when you multiply
the first and last numbers? _____

6. the sum of the first two numbers? _____

7. the sum of the last two numbers? _____

8. the number you get when you subtract
the first number from the last number? _____

More I'm Through! What Can I Do? Grade 3 © 2008 Creative Teaching Press

Name: _____ Date: _____

Magic Number Squares #1

Magic number squares have been around for hundreds of years. In reality, there is nothing "magic" about them. They are simply a pattern of numbers arranged in a manner where all of the rows and columns will add up to the same number. Each number will only appear once in a magic square.

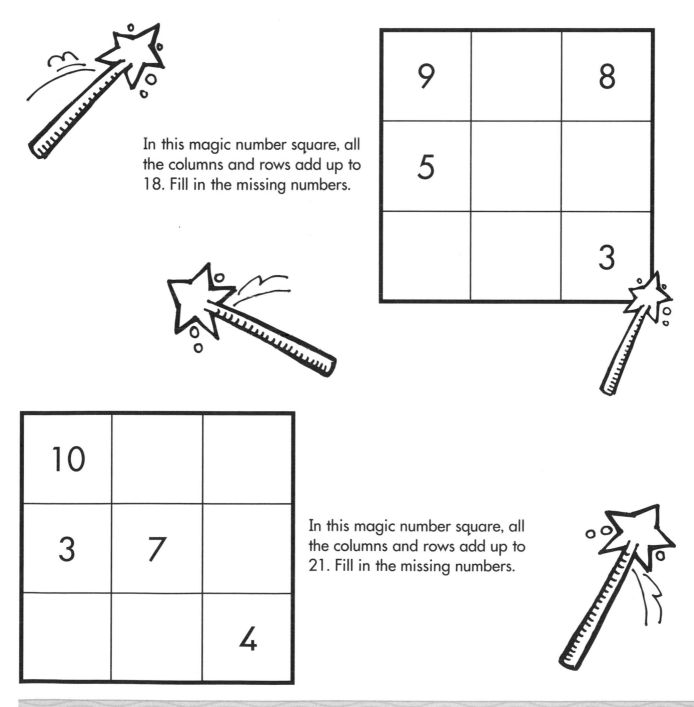

In this magic number square, all the columns and rows add up to 18. Fill in the missing numbers.

9		8
5		
		3

In this magic number square, all the columns and rows add up to 21. Fill in the missing numbers.

10		
3	7	
		4

Magic Number Squares #2

Magic number squares have been around for hundreds of years. In reality, there is nothing "magic" about them. They are simply a pattern of numbers arranged in a manner where all of the rows and columns will add up to the same number. Each number will only appear once in a magic square.

2		
	5	3
6		

In this magic number square, all the columns and rows add up to 15. Fill in the missing numbers.

7		3
	4	
		1

In this magic number square, all the columns and rows add up to 12. Fill in the missing numbers.

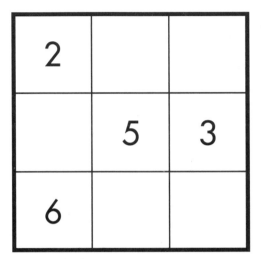

	34	24
	23	

In this magic number square, all the columns and rows add up to 69. Fill in the missing numbers.

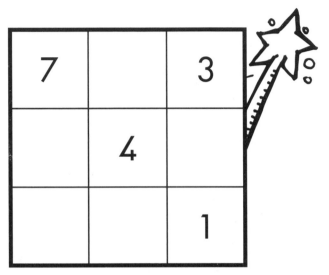

	7	12	13
16		6	
		15	
	14		8

In this magic number square, all the columns and rows add up to 34. Fill in the missing numbers.

More I'm Through! What Can I Do? Grade 3 © 2008 Creative Teaching Press

Expanded Form

Write each number in expanded form. The first one has been started for you.

1. 14,367 = <u>10,000 + 4,000 +   </u>

2. 9,208 = _____

3. 1,029 = _____

4. 594 = _____

Get Ahead

Write one digit in each square to complete the cross–number puzzle.

Across

  A. 5,000 + 300 + 20 + 1

  C. ninety-three

  E. 4 thousands, 3 hundreds,
      6 tens, 7 ones

  G. 10 less than 169

  I. 9,000 + 200

  J. 4 tens

  K. 6,000 + 700 + 3

Down

  A. 50 + 8

  B. one hundred ninety-three

  D. 3 thousands, 6 hundreds,
      1 ten

  E. 100 more than 342

  F. 7 tens, 5 ones

  H. 1 more than 946

  I. 900 + 6

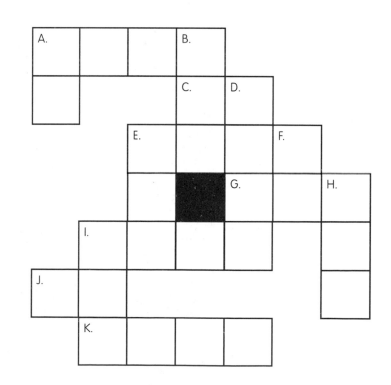

Name: _____   Date: _____

Number Maze #1

Follow the math maze from "Start" to "End." Solve the addition and subtraction problems as you go. Write the final answer in the starburst.

I'm ready to start!

8	+	4		8	+	8
–		–		–		+
4		9		5		6
+		–		–		–
9		4		7		4
–		+		+		+
7		7		9		5
+		–		+		–
8		4		11		4
=		+		–		+
		5	–	7		8

End

Start

More I'm Through! What Can I Do? Grade 3 © 2008 Creative Teaching Press

Number Maze #2

Follow the math maze from "Start" to "End." Solve the
addition, subtraction, multiplication, and division problems
as you go. Write the final answer in the starburst.

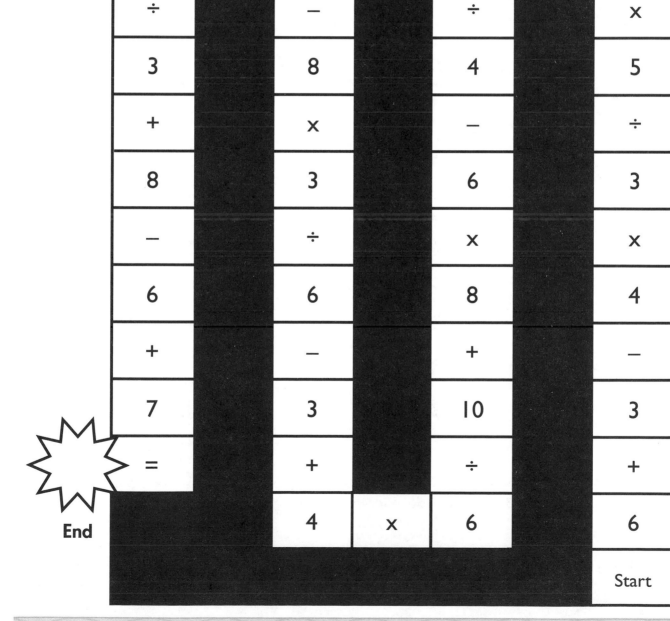

Name: _____   Date: _____

Repeated Addition Superhero

A superhero has special powers that save the day. Multiplication is the "superhero" of addition; its special powers save time when repeated addition is needed.

Problem: $\begin{array}{r} 2 \\ \times 4 \\ \hline \end{array}$ $2 + 2 + 2 + 2 = 8$ 4 sets of two: $\begin{array}{r} 2 \\ 2 \\ 2 \\ + 2 \\ \hline 8 \end{array}$ $4 \times 2 = 8$

Multiply the following numbers. Show the addition problem.

1. **S** $\begin{array}{r} 2 \\ \times 3 \\ \hline 6 \end{array}$

2. **D** $\begin{array}{r} 4 \\ \times 3 \\ \hline \end{array}$

3. **P** $\begin{array}{r} 6 \\ \times 5 \\ \hline \end{array}$

4. **N** $\begin{array}{r} 8 \\ \times 4 \\ \hline \end{array}$

5. **U** $\begin{array}{r} 9 \\ \times 5 \\ \hline \end{array}$

6. **F** $\begin{array}{r} 3 \\ \times 5 \\ \hline \end{array}$

7. **E** $\begin{array}{r} 7 \\ \times 1 \\ \hline \end{array}$

8. **I** $\begin{array}{r} 2 \\ \times 0 \\ \hline \end{array}$

9. **B** $\begin{array}{r} 7 \\ \times 4 \\ \hline \end{array}$

10. **T** $\begin{array}{r} 6 \\ \times 3 \\ \hline \end{array}$

11. **M** $\begin{array}{r} 3 \\ \times 3 \\ \hline \end{array}$

12. **G** $\begin{array}{r} 9 \\ \times 2 \\ \hline \end{array}$

13. **C** $\begin{array}{r} 5 \\ \times 4 \\ \hline \end{array}$

14. **A** $\begin{array}{r} 7 \\ \times 5 \\ \hline \end{array}$

15. **R** $\begin{array}{r} 8 \\ \times 2 \\ \hline \end{array}$

Use your answers to find the name of Sam's favorite superhero. Write the letter that goes with each answer on the lines below. The first one is done for you.

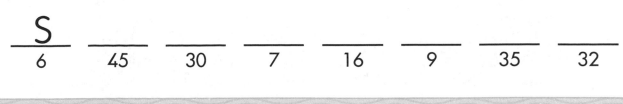

$\underline{\quad S \quad} \ \underline{\qquad} \ \underline{\qquad} \ \underline{\qquad} \ \underline{\qquad} \ \underline{\qquad} \ \underline{\qquad} \ \underline{\qquad}$
  6   45   30   7   16   9   35   32

More I'm Through! What Can I Do? Grade 3 © 2008 Creative Teaching Press

Word Code #1

In this puzzle, each letter of the alphabet is worth a certain amount of points. Which word below is worth the most points? Find out by adding the point value of each letter in the words below. Write the sums on the lines.

Code

A = 1	G = 7	M = 13	S = 19	Y = 25
B = 2	H = 8	N = 14	T = 20	Z = 26
C = 3	I = 9	O = 15	U = 21	
D = 4	J = 10	P = 16	V = 22	
E = 5	K = 11	Q = 17	W = 23	
F = 6	L = 12	R = 18	X = 24	

Example: **if** 15 points   i(9 points) + f(6 points) = 15

1. so _____

2. at _____

3. up _____

4. is _____

5. we _____

6. go _____

7. no _____

8. he _____

The word that is worth the most points is _____ .

Name: _____   Date: _____

Word Code #2

In this puzzle, each letter of the alphabet is worth a certain amount of points. Which word below is worth the most points? Find out by adding the point value of each letter in the words below. Write the sums on the lines.

Code

A = 1	G = 7	M = 13	S = 19	Y = 25
B = 2	H = 8	N = 14	T = 20	Z = 26
C = 3	I = 9	O = 15	U = 21	
D = 4	J = 10	P = 16	V = 22	
E = 5	K = 11	Q = 17	W = 23	
F = 6	L = 12	R = 18	X = 24	

1. knot_____

2. not _____

3. see_____

4. sea _____

5. here_____

6. hear _____

7. son _____

8. sun _____

9. cent_____

10. sent _____

11. blew _____

12. blue_____

13. buy _____

14. bye _____

15. two _____

16. too_____

The word that is worth the most points is _____ .

More I'm Through! What Can I Do? Grade 3 © 2008 Creative Teaching Press

Bingo #1

Use this Bingo card to help you answer the questions below.

	B	I	N	G	O	TOTAL
Row 1	7	18	32	59	70	____
Row 2	15	16	31	50	62	____
Row 3	4	24	FREE	49	74	____
Row 4	9	30	42	47	68	____
Row 5	8	27	39	60	66	____
TOTAL	____	____	____	____	____	

1. Give the total for each row and column on the lines provided above.

2. What is the difference between the totals of the highest and lowest rows? _____

3. What is the difference between the column with the highest total and the row with the lowest total? _____

4. What number would need to be removed from the **I** column to make the total 99? _____

5. How much more does the **G** column total than Row 4? _____

More I'm Through! What Can I Do? Grade 3 © 2008 Creative Teaching Press

Bingo #2

Fill in the Bingo card using the clues below, and then fill in the totals for each row and column on the lines provided.

	B	I	N	G	O	TOTAL
Row 1	6		41		68	_____
Row 2	14	17	34	48		_____
Row 3		22	FREE		74	_____
Row 4	12	30	44	57		_____
Row 5	8		38	46	63	_____
TOTAL	_____	_____	_____	_____	_____	

1. The total of Row 2 is 18 more than Column **N**.

2. Row 4 totals 62 more than the diagonal containing the number 68.

3. Column B totals 297 less than Column **O**.

4. Row 3 totals 3 more than the diagonal containing the number 63.

5. Column **G** and Column **O** total 598.

6. Row 1 totals 16 less than Row 4.

7. Column **I** totals 53 less than Row 2.

More I'm Through! What Can I Do? Grade 3 © 2008 Creative Teaching Press

Solve Our Riddles

Mrs. Marcus's students wrote number riddles and challenged their classmates to solve them. Can you solve them? (**Hint:** Start with the final number and perform each step in reverse order using the opposite operation.) Once you find the beginning number, go back and check your answer by following the steps of the riddle. If you end up with the same final number, you did it correctly.

A. Martin picked his number.
Then he added 254 to it.
Then he divided by 5.
Then he added 12.
His final number was 77.

What was his beginning number? _____

B. Cindy picked her number.
Then she divided by 6.
Then she added 2.
Then she multiplied by 5.
Her final number was 150.

What was her beginning number? _____

C. Tom picked his number.
Then he multiplied by 2.
Then he added 433.
Then he divided by 5.
His final number was 101.

What was his beginning number? _____

D. Leah picked her number.
Then she divided by 12.
Then she added 19.
Then she divided by 9.
Her final number was 3.

What was her beginning number? _____

Name: _____   Date: _____

Magic Multiplication Squares

Multiply the numbers in the middle of the square. Then add the products. All four circles will have the same sum! Look at the example. Then complete the other magic squares. The last square is empty. Make a magic square of your own. (**Hint:** When you multiply by 10, there is always a zero in the one's place: 10 × 2 = 20.)

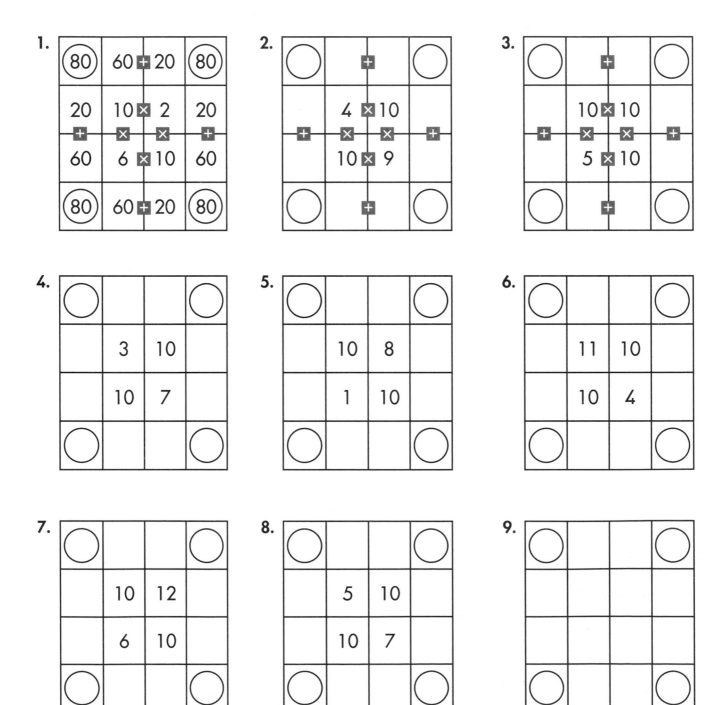

More I'm Through! What Can I Do? Grade 3 © 2008 Creative Teaching Press

It All Adds Up #1

Every row, column, and mini-grid must contain the numbers 1 through 4. The first mini-grid has been done for you.

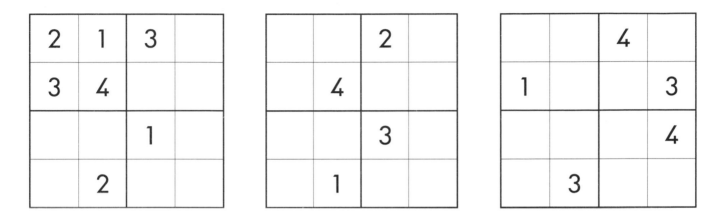

Every row, column, and mini-grid must contain the numbers 1 through 6. The first mini-grid has been done for you.

It All Adds Up #2

Every row, column, and mini-grid must contain the numbers 1 through 9. The first mini-grid has been done for you.

5	7	9		6			2	4
8	4	3	2	9	7	5		
2	1	6	5		4	3		7
	6	8				7	1	
1		7		3		9		5
	9	5		4		2	8	
		4	8		2	1		
9		1	3	5	6	4		2
	5			1			3	

		7		5		3		4
	8	1	4	7	3	5	9	
5			2		6			
7		5		3		4		8
	6	8		4		2		
2		4	9	1		6		7
			3		7			
	5	9	1		4	8	7	
		6		8		1		3

Category Challenge #1

How many words can you think of for each category? Write the words on the lines.

1. Words that end with the letter A (*Example: are<u>a</u>*)

_____   _____

_____   _____

_____   _____

_____   _____

_____   _____

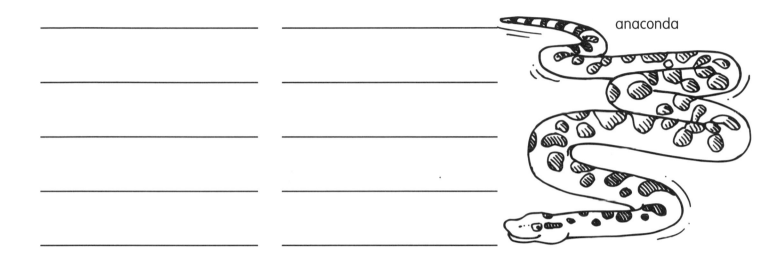

anaconda

2. Words that end with double consonants
(*Example: pu<u>ff</u>*)

puff

_____   _____

_____   _____

_____   _____

_____   _____

_____   _____

Category Challenge #2

How many words can you think of for each category? Write the words on the lines.

1. Begins and ends with S

_____
_____
_____
_____
_____
_____
_____
_____
_____

2. Begins and ends with T

_____
_____
_____
_____
_____
_____
_____
_____
_____

3. Begins and ends with R

_____
_____
_____
_____
_____
_____
_____
_____
_____

4. Begins and ends with A

_____
_____
_____
_____
_____
_____
_____
_____

5. Begins and ends with D

_____
_____
_____
_____
_____
_____
_____
_____

6. Begins and ends with N

_____
_____
_____
_____
_____
_____
_____
_____

More I'm Through! What Can I Do? Grade 3 © 2008 Creative Teaching Press

Day After Day

Solve the following brainteasers. Use a calendar to help you solve them.

1. If today is Wednesday, what will be the day after tomorrow?

_____

2. If two days from today is Thursday, what was yesterday?

_____

3. Yesterday was the 13th. If tomorrow is Wednesday, what will the date be on Saturday?

_____

4. If four days from today will be Monday, what was the day before yesterday?

_____

5. My birthday was five days ago. If three days after tomorrow is the 27th, what was the date of my birthday?

_____

6. Yesterday was Sunday. What was five days before the day after tomorrow?

_____

7. Five days from today will be Friday. What day is four days after tomorrow?

_____

More I'm Through! What Can I Do? Grade 3 © 2008 Creative Teaching Press

What's Next? #1

Color the last shape in each row so that the sequence is continued.

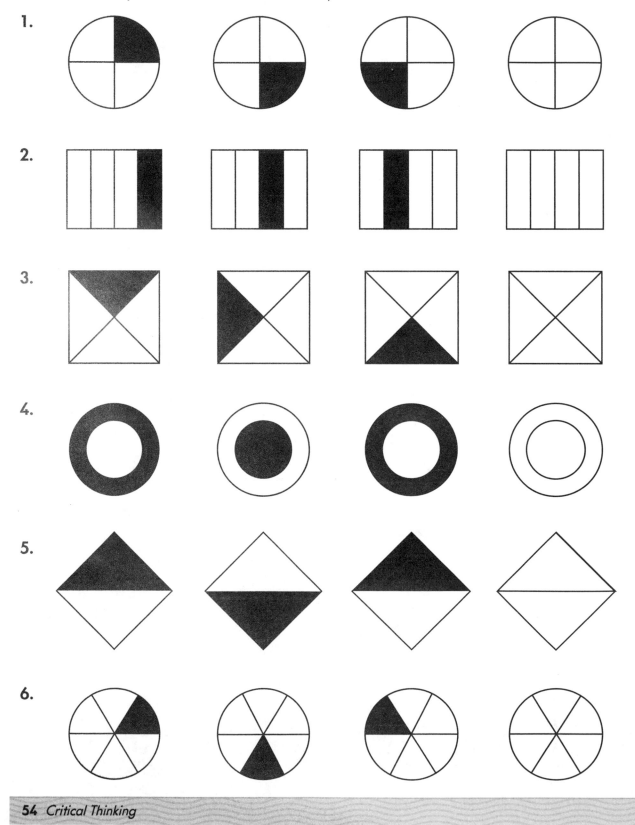

What's Next? #2

Color the last shape in each row so that the sequence is continued.

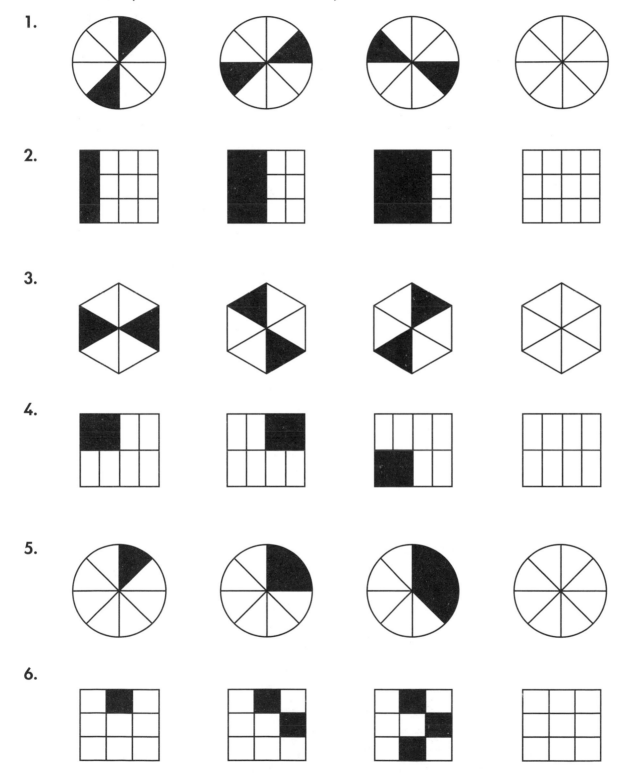

1.

2.

3.

4.

5.

6.

Which Floor?

Five classmates—Neha, Will, Sarah, Katy, and Brodie—live in the same five-story apartment building.

Here are some clues to which floors they live on:

- When Neha visits Will, she has to go down two floors.
- Sarah lives on the floor between Katy and Will.
- When Brodie goes to Neha's to play, he goes up one floor.
- Katy lives on the first floor.

On which floor does each child live?

Neha: _____   Will: _____

Sarah: _____   Katy: _____

Brodie: _____

More I'm Through! What Can I Do? Grade 3 © 2008 Creative Teaching Press

Name: _____   Date: _____

Strain Your Brain

Strain your brain and see how many things you can think of that fit each category. Write your answers in each box.

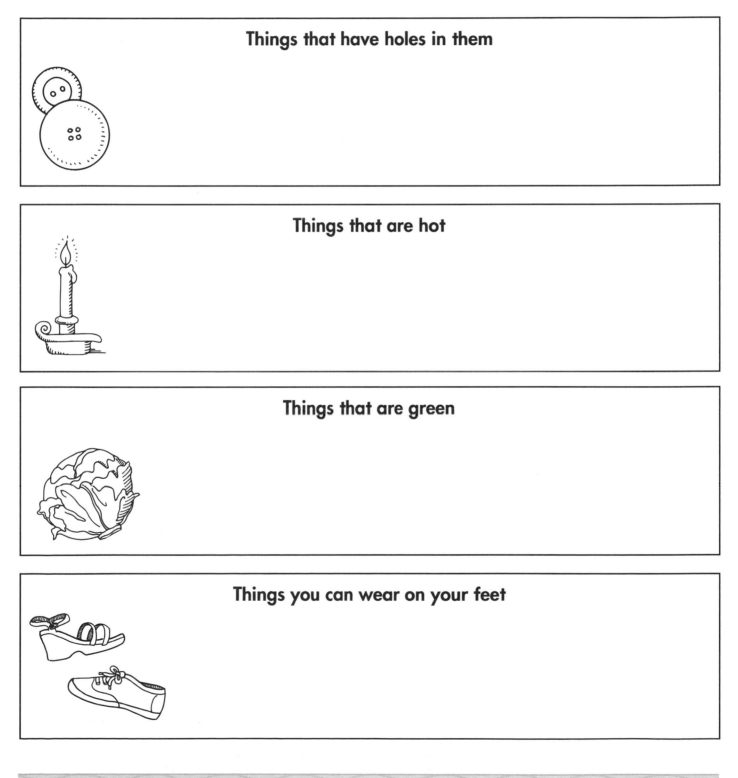

Things that have holes in them

Things that are hot

Things that are green

Things you can wear on your feet

Name: _____   Date: _____

Animal Ad-VENN-tures

How many animal names can you think of that fit in each of the numbered sections on this Venn diagram? Be careful—each word can be correctly placed in only one section.

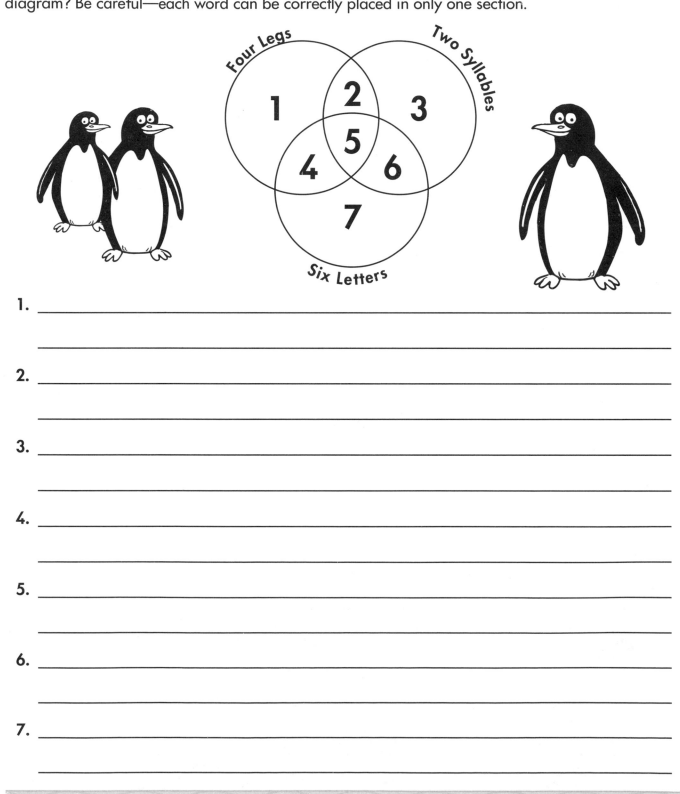

1. _____
   _____

2. _____
   _____

3. _____
   _____

4. _____
   _____

5. _____
   _____

6. _____
   _____

7. _____
   _____

More I'm Through! What Can I Do? Grade 3 © 2008 Creative Teaching Press

More Ad-VENN-tures

How many words can you think of that fit in each of the numbered sections of this Venn diagram? Be careful—each word can be correctly placed in only one section.

1. _____

_____

2. _____

_____

3. _____

_____

4. _____

_____

5. _____

_____

6. _____

_____

7. _____

_____

Geometry Puzzle

Using the letters and the circle, the triangle, the square, and the rectangle, write the answers to the questions.

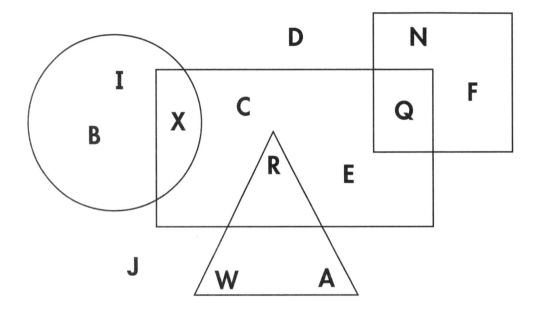

1. Which letters are in the square only? _____

2. Which letter is in the square and the rectangle? _____

3. Which letter is in the triangle and the rectangle? _____

4. Which letter is in the circle and the rectangle? _____

5. Which letters are in the triangle only? _____

6. Which letters are in the circle only? _____

7. Which letters are in the rectangle only? _____

8. Which letters are not in the rectangle, circle, triangle, or square? _____

More I'm Through! What Can I Do? Grade 3 © 2008 Creative Teaching Press

Volunteer Jobs

Curtis, Linda, Lin, Yonni, and Collin are all volunteering at the zoo this summer. Their jobs are selling tickets, cleaning cages, feeding animals, sweeping sidewalks, and selling snacks. Use the clues to match each child to the correct job.

- Curtis wears old clothes so he won't get dirty on his job.
- Linda serves drinks as part of her job.
- Lin has to be able to count money and make change for her job.
- Yonni has to remember which animal likes bananas.
- Collin uses soap and water on his job.

	Selling Tickets	Cleaning Cages	Feeding Animals	Sweeping Sidewalks	Selling Snacks
Curtis					
Linda					
Lin					
Yonni					
Collin					

Animal Scramble

Rearrange the letters in each word below, add one letter, and you will find the name of an animal!

Example: red + e = deer

1. are _____

2. dot _____

3. meal _____

4. tire _____

5. rash _____

6. pride _____

7. sore _____

8. parole _____

9. bare _____

10. mall _____

11. master _____

12. some _____

13. oil _____

14. brave _____

15. sank _____

More I'm Through! What Can I Do? Grade 3 © 2008 Creative Teaching Press

Odd Word Out

In each row, all of the words have something in common except one. Find and circle the word that does not belong in each row. The first one has been done for you.

1. two   six   four   (time)   ten

2. blue   blew   green   black   yellow

3. tulip   rose   tree   daisy   pansy

4. broccoli   apple   peach   grape   banana

5. eye   nose   foot   ear   mouth

6. owl   robin   hawk   salmon   sparrow

7. square   vase   circle   triangle   rectangle

8. shoe   jacket   slipper   boot   sandal

9. sofa   chair   couch   bench   dresser

10. bee   lizard   ant   beetle   wasp

11. bright   happy   lazy   toward   thick

12. invite   wobble   grow   think   desk

Identify the Shapes

Color each shape as follows:

octagon: purple

trapezoid: brown

oval: green

triangle: blue

hexagon: orange

pentagon: yellow

circle: pink

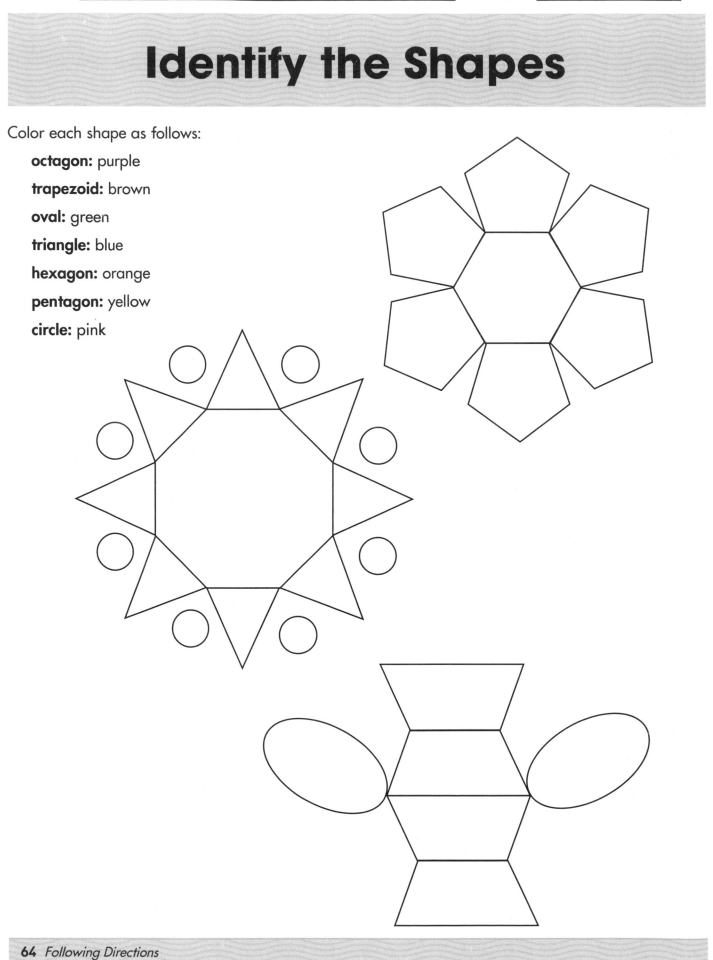

More I'm Through! What Can I Do? Grade 3 © 2008 Creative Teaching Press

Solve the Riddle

Follow the directions to find the answer to the riddle.

How do you keep a skunk from smelling?

- Write the letter **a** on line 6.
- Write the word **plug** on line 2.
- Write the word **with** on line 5.
- Write the word **You** on line 1.
- Write the word **its** on line 3.
- Write the word **clothespin** on line 7.
- Write the word **nose** on line 4.

1. _____

2. _____

3. _____

4. _____

5. _____

6. _____

7. _____

More I'm Through! What Can I Do? Grade 3 © 2008 Creative Teaching Press

Graph a Giraffe

Using a ruler and the grid on page 67, draw straight lines to connect the grid points below in the order given. You will create a picture of a giraffe. The first lines have been drawn for you.

1. W-11	W-5	V-5	T-10	U-11		
2. U-11	U-22	P-27	O-23	V-2		
3. V-2	T-2	Q-13	N-21	M-22		
4. M-22	L-13	M-2	K-2	K-23		
5. K-23	I-23	G-23	F-19	C-12		
6. C-12	D-2	B-2	B-14	C-16	C-30	
7. I-23	I-19	F-12	G-2	E-2	E-14	F-19
8. C-30	N-35	X-23	W-11			

More I'm Through! What Can I Do? Grade 3 © 2008 Creative Teaching Press

Name: _____   Date: _____

Graph a Giraffe (cont.)

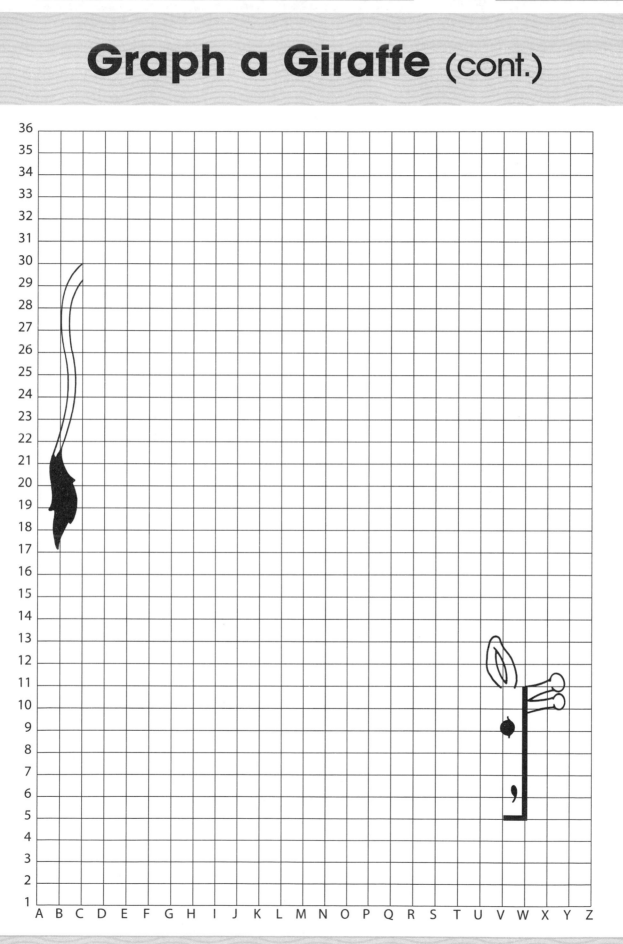

Color the Train

A train is hidden in the squares below. To find it, color all of the squares with even numbers blue. Color all of the squares with odd numbers yellow.

15	1	3	17	25	41	9	13	23	47	69
47	27	89	11	19	39	77	37	61	11	29
63	5	21	7	91	83	35	91	75	53	29
73	57	8	16	22	48	77	10	54	20	86
85	71	43	18	60	87	91	22	93	24	94
99	3	33	26	32	5	37	80	9	32	13
25	47	34	36	42	40	84	76	46	98	21
23	52	68	54	56	50	32	64	86	66	45
31	27	52	70	74	58	36	24	68	44	21
37	86	90	88	84	44	96	38	88	98	11
14	8	12	26	40	4	20	6	18	46	33
59	61	63	66	42	73	85	22	52	75	53
8	591	83	25	71	25	49	65	3	81	13
9	23	11	45	95	47	31	61	35	11	3
47	33	89	53	21	93	41	85	97	91	51
31	43	55	7	33	5	51	15	71	21	87

More I'm Through! What Can I Do? Grade 3 © 2008 Creative Teaching Press

Riddle Time #1

Follow the directions below to solve the riddle. The first step has been done for you.

What did the archaeologist say to the mummy?

LAZY	~~CALVES~~	THERE	NOSE
NERVOUS	LIBRARIAN	~~CITIES~~	I
HELPFUL	DIG	MOUTH	NURSE
YOU	THEY'RE	EYE	~~WISHES~~

1. Cross off all words that are plurals.
2. Cross off all words that name a part of the face.
3. Cross off all words that are homophones for the word *their*.
4. Cross off all words that are adjectives.
5. Cross off all words that are the names of community helpers.

The words that have **NOT** been crossed off are the answer to the riddle.

- Draw a circle around each of these words.
- Start in the top left-hand corner of the puzzle.
- Read the circled words going **across** each row.
- Write the answer to the riddle on the line below.

More I'm Through! What Can I Do? Grade 3 © 2008 Creative Teaching Press

Riddle Time #2

Follow the directions below to solve the riddle.

Why did the squirrel stop arguing with the porcupine?

LENTIL	BROOK	CHECKERS	LION
HOMEWORK	APPLE	DELICIOUS	HIGH
CAB	NECKTIE	CHESS	EXCITING
SHE	CARDS	GOT	ZEBRA
THE	SAILBOAT	OLD	POINT

1. Cross off all words that are compound words.
2. Cross off all words that are adjectives.
3. Cross off all words that are names of games people play.
4. Cross off all words that are names of zoo animals.
5. Cross off all words that come **before** the word *cable* in the dictionary.
6. Cross off all words that begin and end with the same letter.

The words that have **NOT** been crossed off are the answer to the riddle.

- Draw a circle around each of these words.
- Start in the top left-hand corner of the puzzle.
- Read the circled words going **across** each row.
- Write the answer to the riddle on the line below.

_____

More I'm Through! What Can I Do? Grade 3 © 2008 Creative Teaching Press

Cinquain Poem

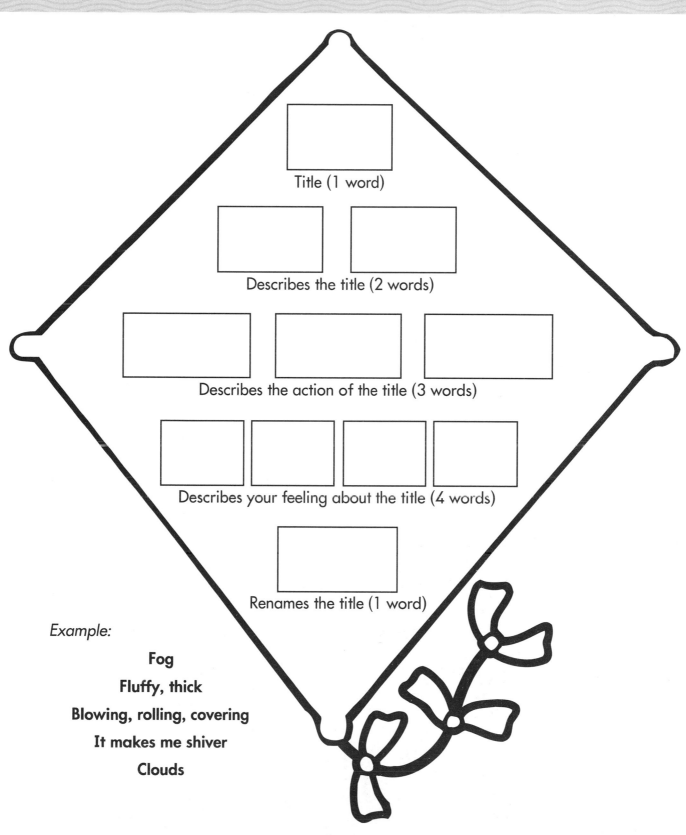

Title (1 word)

Describes the title (2 words)

Describes the action of the title (3 words)

Describes your feeling about the title (4 words)

Renames the title (1 word)

Example:

Fog

Fluffy, thick

Blowing, rolling, covering

It makes me shiver

Clouds

More I'm Through! What Can I Do? Grade 3 © 2008 Creative Teaching Press

Diamonte Poem

_____
(noun)

_____   _____
(adjective)   (adjective)

_____   _____   _____
(verb ending in -ing)   (verb ending in -ing)   (verb ending in -ing)

_____ _____ _____ _____
(noun)   (noun)   (noun)   (noun)

_____   _____   _____
(verb ending in -ing)   (verb ending in -ing)   (verb ending in -ing)

_____   _____
(adjective)   (adjective)

_____
(noun)

Example:

Snake
scaly, sneaky
slithering, sliding, biting
boa, reptile, predator, bird
flying, soaring, floating
brown, feathered
Eagle

_____
(noun)

_____   _____
(adjective)   (adjective)

_____   _____   _____
(verb ending in -ing)   (verb ending in -ing)   (verb ending in -ing)

_____ _____ _____ _____
(noun)   (noun)   (noun)   (noun)

_____   _____   _____
(verb ending in -ing)   (verb ending in -ing)   (verb ending in -ing)

_____   _____
(adjective)   (adjective)

_____
(noun)

More I'm Through! What Can I Do? Grade 3 © 2008 Creative Teaching Press

What's My Name?

FqPrdtixaxd   aPgqztzax

Follow each step in order to find the name of a famous explorer. Write your final answer on the lines at the bottom of the page.

1. Change all the x's to n's.

2. Cross out all the P's.

3. Add an M to the beginning of the second word.

4. Change all the q's to e's.

5. Change all the z's to l's.

6. Cross out all the t's.

The explorer is

___ ___ ___ ___ ___ ___ ___ ___

___ ___ ___ ___ ___ ___ ___ ___

More I'm Through! What Can I Do? Grade 3 © 2008 Creative Teaching Press

Draw a Monkey

1. Draw the body and head of the monkey.

2. Draw curves for the face and stomach. Add arms and legs as shown.

3. Draw the feet, ears, and hands. Erase the dotted lines.

4. Add eyebrows, eyes, a nose, a mouth, and a tail.

Draw two monkeys here. Draw a banana in each monkey's hand.

More I'm Through! What Can I Do? Grade 3 © 2008 Creative Teaching Press

Name: _____   Date: _____

Draw a Fire Engine

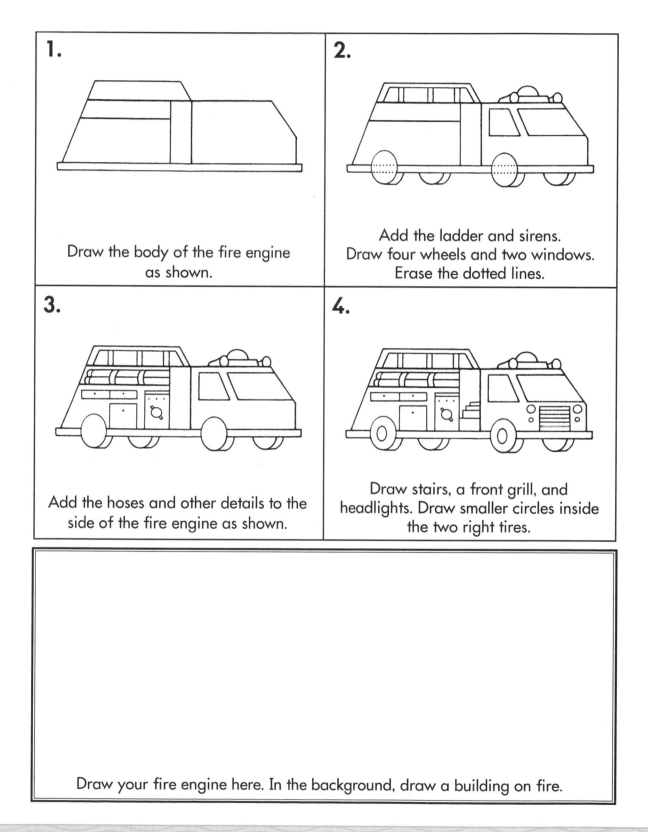

1.

Draw the body of the fire engine
as shown.

2.

Add the ladder and sirens.
Draw four wheels and two windows.
Erase the dotted lines.

3.

Add the hoses and other details to the
side of the fire engine as shown.

4.

Draw stairs, a front grill, and
headlights. Draw smaller circles inside
the two right tires.

Draw your fire engine here. In the background, draw a building on fire.

Best in Show

Which dog on page 77 won Best in Show? To find out, read the judges' comments and cross off one dog at a time until only one is left.

The dog that won does not have exactly five letters in its name.

The dog that won does not have a name that is a compound word.

The winning dog does not have a name that rhymes with the word *noodle*.

The winning dog does not have a name with two identical consonants in the middle.

The winning dog does not have the name of a continent in its name.

The dog that won does not have exactly fifteen letters in its name.

The last five letters of the winning dog do not spell the name of a bird.

The winning dog does not have a name that starts and ends with consonants.

The dog judges picked for Best in Show was the _____.

Best in Show (cont.)

Poodle

Cocker Spaniel

Golden Retriever

Chihuahua

Australian Shepherd

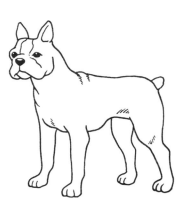

Boxer

Collie

Bloodhound

Beagle

Repeated Patterns

What comes next?

Draw the next three images in each pattern.

1. 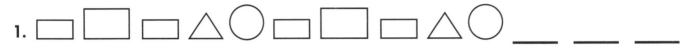 ___ ___ ___

2. A B D C A B D C A ___ ___ ___ ___

3. ☆ ◯ ☆ ▢ ☆ ◯ ☆ ▢ ☆ ___ ___ ___

4. snap clap tap snap clap tap ___ ___ ___

5. + ÷ × = + ÷ × = + ÷ ___ ___ ___

6. ___ ___ ___

More I'm Through! What Can I Do? Grade 3 © 2008 Creative Teaching Press

Name: _____   Date: _____

Connect the Line Segments

Draw each line segment using a straightedge.

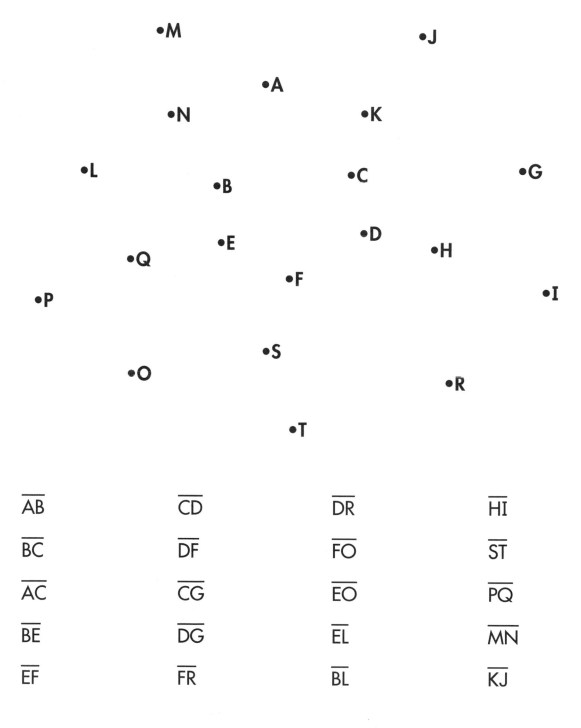

$\overline{AB}$	$\overline{CD}$	$\overline{DR}$	$\overline{HI}$
$\overline{BC}$	$\overline{DF}$	$\overline{FO}$	$\overline{ST}$
$\overline{AC}$	$\overline{CG}$	$\overline{EO}$	$\overline{PQ}$
$\overline{BE}$	$\overline{DG}$	$\overline{EL}$	$\overline{MN}$
$\overline{EF}$	$\overline{FR}$	$\overline{BL}$	$\overline{KJ}$

What picture did you create? _____

Name: _____   Date: _____

Dot-to-Dot Vehicle

Connect the dots counting by 2s to discover a hidden vehicle.

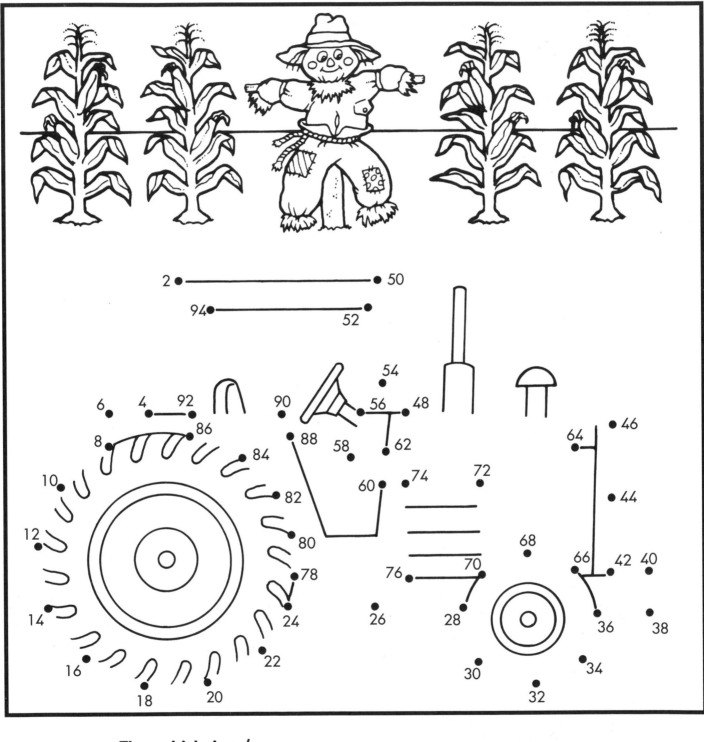

The vehicle is a/an _____.

More I'm Through! What Can I Do? Grade 3 © 2008 Creative Teaching Press

Cat and Mouse Dialogue

Write a dialogue between the cat and mouse in these pictures.

Between Friends Dialogue

Write a dialogue between the two friends in these pictures.

Help the Dog Maze

Help the dog find his way to the bone!

Help the Ant Maze

Help the ant find its way back to the anthill!

More I'm Through! What Can I Do? Grade 3 © 2008 Creative Teaching Press

Crack the Code #1

Use the code below to find the answers to the riddles. Write the letters that match the symbols on the lines.

A	B	C	D	E	F	G	H	I	J	K	L	M
●	◄	☯	□	★	☺	◉	&	☾	♊	☼	➤	✓

N	O	P	Q	R	S	T	U	V	W	X	Y	Z
⚑	👍	●	❀	⊠	∿	♈	♓	◆	◇	❖	✻	➤

Riddle #1

What did the guitar say to the famous rock star?

◇ & ✻   ● ⊠ ★   ✻ 👍 ♓   ● ➤ ◇ ● ✻ ∿

___ ___ ___   ___ ___ ___   ___ ___ ___   ___ ___ ___ ___ ___ ___

♦ ☾ ☯● ☼ ☾ ⚑◉   👍 ⚑   ✓ ★

___ ___ ___ ___ ___ ___ ___   ___ ___   ___ ___

___ ___ ___ ___ ___ ___ ___   ___ ___ ___?

Riddle #2

Why did the man put his car in the oven?

& ★   ◇ ● ⚑ ♈ ★ □   ●

___ ___   ___ ___ ___ ___ ___ ___   ___

& 👍 ♈   ⊠ 👍 □

___ ___ ___   ___ ___ ___

___ ___ ___ ___ ___ ___ ___.

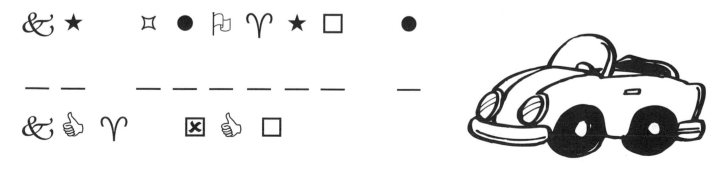

More I'm Through! What Can I Do? Grade 3 © 2008 Creative Teaching Press

Crack the Code #2

Use the code below to find the answers to the riddles. Write the letters that match the symbols on the lines.

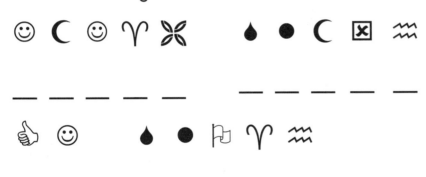

Riddle #1
What has 100 legs?

☺ ☾ ☺ ♈ ❀   💧 ● ☾ ⊠ ≋

__ __ __ __ __   __ __ __ __ __

👍 ☺   💧 ● 🏳 ♈ ≋

__ __   __ __ __ __ __ .

Riddle #2
Why did the little bat brush his teeth?

& ★   & ● ▢

__ __   __ __ __

◄ ● ♈   ◄ ⊠ ★ ● ♈ &

__ __ __   __ __ __ __ __ __ .

More I'm Through! What Can I Do? Grade 3 © 2008 Creative Teaching Press

Crack the Code #3

Use the code below to find the answers to the riddles. Write the letters that match the symbols on the lines.

A	B	C	D	E	F	G	H	I	J	K	L	M
●	◄	☯	□	★	☺	◉	&	☾	♊	✷	➤	✓

N	O	P	Q	R	S	T	U	V	W	X	Y	Z
⚐	👍	🌢	✿	☒	〰	♈	♓	◆	◇	❖	✤	➤

Riddle #1
Why did the boy bring a ladder to his middle school?

& ★   ✦ ● ⚐ ♈ ★ □   ♈ 👍   ◄ ★

___ ___   ___ ___ ___ ___ ___ ___   ___ ___   ___ ___

☾ ⚐   & ☾ ◉ &   〰 ☯ & 👍 👍 ➤

___ ___   ___ ___ ___ ___   ___ ___ ___ ___ ___ ___ .

Riddle #2
Where does the magician keep his rabbit?

☾ ⚐   ●   ♈ 👍 🌢   & ● ♈

___ ___   ___   ___ ___ ___   ___ ___ ___ .

Complete the Teddy Bear

Draw the other half of the teddy bear to match the side that is completed. Color your teddy bear.

More I'm Through! What Can I Do? Grade 3 © 2008 Creative Teaching Press

Name: _____ Date: _____

Complete the House

Draw the other half of the house to match the side that is completed. Color your house.

Complete the Zoo Entrance

Draw the other half of the zoo entrance to match the side that is completed. Color your zoo entrance.

More I'm Through! What Can I Do? Grade 3 © 2008 Creative Teaching Press

Complete the King

Draw the other half of the king to match the side that is completed. Color your king.

Answer Key

Magic Word Square #1 (Page 5)
Possible answers include:

awning	nap	sap	spin
can	nip	saw	swan
cap	pain	scan	swap
casing	pan	sign	wag
gain	paw	sin	was
gap	pawn	sing	wasp
gas	pin	spa	
gasp	sac	span	
nag	sag	spawn	

Magic Word Square #2 (Page 6)
Possible answers include:

age	gal	loan	plea
agent	gate	lone	plot
ale	gel	long	pole
aloe	get	lot	polo
alone	gnat	nag	tag
along	kale	neat	take
alp	key	net	taken
angel	lag	not	tale
ant	lake	oak	talk
ate	lane	oat	talon
eat	leak	one	tan
eaten	leaky	pea	tea
eel	lean	peak	ten
elegant	leek	plan	tent
elk	leg	lane	toe
elongate	lent	planet	ton
elope	let	plant	tone

Magic Word Square #3 (Page 7)
Possible answers include:

chip	hill	move	silk
clip	hip	oil	silver
eel	hire	pail	sip
eve	hiss	palm	size
eves	hit	pals	skip
evil	hive	pave	slam
film	ill	pie	slap
flip	lice	pig	slave
hail	lid	pike	slice
halve	lie	pile	slid
have	life	pill	slide
heal	like	pills	slim
heap	lime	pine	slime
heel	limp	pin	slum
help	line	pipe	snip
hem	lips	pit	soil
hen	lisp	sail	solve
her	list	save	this
hers	live	ship	veil
hide	love	side	whip
hike	mail	sigh	

Magic Word Square #4 (Page 8)
Possible answers include:

begin	gone	nod	owe
coin	grin	noise	oxen
doing	hinge	none	ozone
dozen	icon	noon	pigeon
end	into	nose	region
ending	iron	note	ring
engine	join	noun	sign
gain	king	oink	sing
gaze	lion	once	union
gene	loin	onion	wing
give	neon	ooze	zero
given	nice	open	zone
going	nine	oven	

Fun Words (Page 9)
Answers will vary.

Rhyming Word Robot (Page 10)
The robot should be colored as follows:
red—rake, make, lake
yellow—greet, wheat, meat, feet
green—sing, wing
brown—test, rest, guest, nest
orange—light, fight
blue—plot, got
purple—play, tray, say
black—fit, quit

Mammals Word Scramble (Page 11)

tiger	panda	giraffe
squirrel	kangaroo	camel
hamster	gorilla	elephant
skunk	polar bear	horse
zebra	raccoon	sheep

They are always spotted.

Outer Space Word Scramble (Page 12)

planet	spaceship	meteor
stars	astronaut	comet
moon	galaxy	
sun	asteroid	

Flying saucers

Around the House Word Scramble (Page 13)

bedroom	television	table
kitchen	stove	sink
sofa	windows	
bathroom	toilet	

One with no springs

Common Things (Page 14)
Answers will vary.

Draw the Noun (Page 15)
Drawings will vary. Check for accuracy.

Short u Words (Page 16)

crutches	cub	sun
scrub	plump	lunch
tub	fun	jump
plum	crust	gum

The following words should be circled in the word search puzzle:

at	hat	sit
ax	hot	thick
cot	on	
has	ox	

Weather Word Search (Page 17)

Simple Machines Word Search (Page 18)

Bodies of Water and Landforms Word Search (Page 19)

Mixed Analogies Word Search (Page 20)

1. left
2. night
3. metal
4. soup
5. head
6. flies
7. people
8. red
9. plane
10. county
11. bear
12. sty

```
G T E N I C I D E M C X B
R A E B R V E L P O E P W
S P H U R K S W O O D R S
Y N X A E T I S Y P K I O
T F P B D U F L E F T Q U
N T L E C A A G J M H C P
U L A I D T F H W E G R D
O O N E E P F S A N I D Y
C I E M E S M D G H N K T
M O T A D P O L E B Z A S
```

Television Word Detective (page 21)

Possible answers include:

eel	list	oven	stove
else	lit	see	ten
elves	live	seen	tie
even	lose	sent	tile
event	lost	set	tin
evil	lot	seven	toe
into	love	silent	ton
invite	nest	sit	tonsil
its	net	soil	vest
lens	noise	solve	vet
let	nose	son	vine
lies	not	steel	violin
line	note	stole	vision
lint	oil	stolen	visit
lion	one	stone	vote

Communities Word Detective (Page 22)

Possible answers include:

cent	item	nice	stem
cities	men	nicest	stone
coin	menu	noise	suit
come	met	not	sum
comet	mice	note	sun
comment	mine	notice	ten
cone	mint	nut	tie
cost	minus	once	time
costume	minutes	one	tin
cot	moist	ounce	toe
count	mom	out	ton
cousin	moment	scent	tone
custom	most	scout	tune
cut	mouse	section	unit
cute	music	set	untie
ice	must	since	use
insect	nest	sit	
into	net	some	

Solar System Word Detective (Page 23)

Possible answers include:

alert	lose	oar	sort
almost	loser	oat	star
also	loss	rat	stare
alter	lost	rate	stay
are	lot	ray	steal
arm	male	rest	steam
army	malt	roam	stem
art	mass	roast	stole
ear	master	role	store
early	mat	rose	storm
east	mate	royal	story
easy	mats	sale	stream
eat	mayor	salt	tale
essay	meal	same	team
laser	meat	say	tear
last	melt	seal	toe
late	mess	seat	tore
later	messy	set	toss
lay	metal	slam	toy
layer	mole	smart	toys
least	more	soar	tray
less	most	some	year
let	mostly	sore	

Family Similes (Page 24)

Answers will vary.

Metaphor Medley (Page 25)

Possible answers include:

1. No. Sammy's father is very strong like Hercules.
2. No. Sherrie was very spoiled like a princess.
3. No. The football player was charging very quickly like a bull.
4. No. The student's achievements were bright like a star.
5. No. The child was acting silly like a clown.

Word Blocks (Page 26)

Possible answers include:

blew	coy	sew
blow	fashion	snow
boil	flaw	soil
book	flew	sought
bought	flow	sow
bow	law	soy
boy	look	taught
buy	low	took
caught	new	tow
coil	now	toy
cook	raw	
cow	row	

Plurals Crossword Puzzle (Page 27)

Across
3. foxes
5. babies
7. children
9. mice
11. calves
13. geese
15. halves
16. tomatoes

Down
1. women
2. donkeys
4. tools
6. bunnies
8. heroes
10. cargoes
12. altos
14. men

Five Senses Poem (Page 28)

Poems will vary.

At School Word Links (Page 29)

1. test
2. desk
3. student
4. ruler
5. pencil
6. glue
7. recess
8. eraser
9. notebook
10. board
11. lesson
12. office
13. scissors
14. binder
15. spelling
16. computer
17. crayon
18. study
19. homework
20. science

States Word Links (Page 30)

1. Alabama or Alaska
2. Delaware
3. Texas
4. Ohio
5. Maryland
6. Hawaii
7. Vermont
8. Montana
9. Iowa
10. Oregon
11. Idaho
12. Arizona
13. Washington
14. Georgia
15. Alabama or Alaska
16. New York
17. Mississippi
18. Wyoming
19. Nevada
20. Wisconsin

Ship's Path to 50 (Page 31)

3	2	3	4	5	6	7
6	2	4	0	3	2	1
9	3	6	4	0	1	2
4	5	2	1	5	6	7
3	2	4	3	9	9	8
4	7	6	7	2	1	4
9	7	5	1	4	3	0
2	1	3	2	3	4	2
4	3	6	3	9	7	5
7	2	4	4	0	5	9
2	4	1	0	6	0	8

$3 + 6 + 9 + 4 + 5 + 2 + 1 + 3 + 7 + 1 + 2 + 3 + 4 + 0$

Ship's Path to 84 (Page 32)

3	2	3	4	5	6	7
6	2	4	0	3	2	1
9	3	6	4	0	1	2
4	5	2	1	5	6	7
3	2	4	3	9	9	8
4	7	6	7	2	1	4
9	7	5	1	4	3	0
2	1	3	2	3	4	2
4	3	6	3	9	7	5
7	2	4	4	0	5	9
2	4	1	0	6	0	8

3 + 6 + 9 + 4 + 5 + 2 + 1 + 3 + 7 + 1 + 5 + 7 + 9 + 2 + 4 + 3 + 6 + 3 + 4 + 0

Addition and Subtraction Riddle #1 (Page 33)

1. 6
2. 15
3. 8
4. 24
5. 31
6. 10
7. 14
8. 12
9. 9
10. 23
11. 7
12. 41

A deck of cards

Addition and Subtraction Riddle #2 (Page 34)

1. 26
2. 5
3. 10
4. 21
5. 20
6. 100
7. 4
8. 22
9. 7
10. 25
11. 13
12. 63

Corn on the cob

Ice Cream Numbers (Page 35)

1. 259
2. 952
3. 14
4. 3
5. 45
6. 11
7. 7
8. 4

Clipboard Numbers (Page 36)

1. 368
2. 863
3. 14
4. 5
5. 48
6. 9
7. 11
8. 2

Magic Number Squares #1 (Page 37)

9	1	8
5	6	7
4	11	3

10	5	6
3	7	11
8	9	4

Magic Number Squares #2 (Page 38)

2	9	4
7	5	3
6	1	8

7	2	3
0	4	8
5	6	1

11	34	24
36	23	10
22	12	35

2	7	12	13
16	9	6	3
5	4	15	10
11	14	1	8

Expanded Form (Page 39)

1. 10,000 + 4,000 + 300 + 60 + 7
2. 9,000 + 200 + 8
3. 1,000 + 20 + 9
4. 500 + 90 + 4

Across
A. 5,321
C. 93
E. 4,367
G. 159
I. 9,200
J. 40
K. 6,703

Down
A. 58
B. 193
D. 3,610
E. 442
F. 75
H. 947
I. 906

Number Maze #1 (Page 40)

19

Number Maze #2 (Page 41)

10

Repeated Addition Superhero (Page 42)

1. 6; 2 + 2 + 2 = 6
2. 12; 3 + 3 + 3 + 3 = 12
3. 30; 5 + 5 + 5 + 5 + 5 + 5 = 30
4. 32; 4 + 4 + 4 + 4 + 4 + 4 + 4 + 4 = 32
5. 45; 5 + 5 + 5 + 5 + 5 + 5 + 5 + 5 + 5 = 45
6. 15; 5 + 5 + 5 = 15
7. 7; 1 + 1 + 1 + 1 + 1 + 1 + 1 = 7
8. 0; 0 + 0 = 0
9. 28; 4 + 4 + 4 + 4 + 4 + 4 + 4 = 28
10. 18; 3 + 3 + 3 + 3 + 3 + 3 = 18
11. 9; 3 + 3 + 3 = 9
12. 18; 2 + 2 + 2 + 2 + 2 + 2 + 2 + 2 + 2 = 18
13. 20; 4 + 4 + 4 + 4 + 4 = 20
14. 35; 5 + 5 + 5 + 5 + 5 + 5 + 5 = 35
15. 16; 2 + 2 + 2 + 2 + 2 + 2 + 2 + 2 = 16

Superman

Word Code #1 (Page 43)

1. so = 34
2. at = 21
3. up = 37
4. is = 28
5. we = 28
6. go = 22
7. no = 29
8. he = 13

up (#3) is worth the most points (37)

Word Code #2 (Page 44)

1. knot = 60
2. not = 49
3. see = 29
4. sea = 25
5. here = 36
6. hear = 32
7. son = 48
8. sun = 54
9. cent = 42
10. sent = 58
11. blew = 42
12. blue = 40
13. buy = 48
14. bye = 32
15. two = 58
16. too = 50

knot (#1) is worth the most points (60)

Bingo #1 (Page 45)

1. Row 1: 186
   Row 2: 174
   Row 3: 151
   Row 4: 196
   Row 5: 200
   Column B: 43
   Column I: 115
   Column N: 144
   Column G: 265
   Column O: 340
2. 49
3. 189
4. 16
5. 69

Bingo #2 (Page 46)

Fill-ins:
Row 1: 25, 60
Row 2: 62
Row 3: 3, 47
Row 4: 73
Row 5: 28

Totals:
Row 1 = 200
Row 2 = 175
Row 3 = 146
Row 4 = 216
Row 5 = 183
Column B = 43
Column I = 122
Column N = 157
Column G = 258
Column O = 340

Solve Our Riddles (Page 47)

A. 71
B. 168
C. 36
D. 96

Magic Multiplication Squares (Page 48)

2.

130	40	90	130
40	4	10	40
90	10	9	90
130	40	90	130

3.

150	50	100	150
100	10	10	100
50	5	10	50
150	50	100	150

4.

100	30	70	100
30	3	10	30
70	10	7	70
100	30	70	100

5.

90	10	80	90
80	10	8	80
10	1	10	10
90	10	80	90

6.

150	110	40	150
110	11	10	110
40	10	4	40
150	110	40	150

7.

180	60	120	180
120	10	12	120
60	6	10	60
180	60	120	180

8.

120	50	70	120
50	5	10	50
70	10	7	70
120	50	70	120

9. Answers will vary.

It All Adds Up #1 (Page 49)

2	1	3	4
3	4	2	1
4	3	1	2
1	2	4	3

1	3	2	4
2	4	1	3
4	2	3	1
3	1	4	2

3	2	4	1
1	4	2	3
2	1	3	4
4	3	1	2

2	1	5	6	4	3
6	3	4	5	1	2
4	5	6	2	3	1
1	2	3	4	6	5
5	6	1	3	2	4
3	4	2	1	5	6

6	1	2	4	5	3
4	3	5	6	1	2
5	2	6	1	3	4
3	4	1	2	6	5
1	5	4	3	2	6
2	6	3	5	4	1

It All Adds Up #2 (Page 50)

5	7	9	1	6	3	8	2	4
8	4	3	2	9	7	5	6	1
2	1	6	5	8	4	3	9	7
4	6	8	9	2	5	7	1	3
1	2	7	6	3	8	9	4	5
3	9	5	7	4	1	2	8	6
6	3	4	8	7	2	1	5	9
9	8	1	3	5	6	4	7	2
7	5	2	4	1	9	6	3	8

9	2	7	8	5	1	3	6	4
6	8	1	4	7	3	5	9	2
5	4	3	2	9	6	7	8	1
7	9	5	6	3	2	4	1	8
1	6	8	7	4	5	2	3	9
2	3	4	9	1	8	6	5	7
8	1	2	3	6	7	9	4	5
3	5	9	1	2	4	8	7	6
4	7	6	5	8	9	1	2	3

Category Challenge #1 (Page 51)

Possible answers include:
1. area, sea, arena, spa, tea, pea, boa, plea, lava, data
2. grass, hiss, class, huff, puff, cuff, tall, mall, ball, call, pill, shall, mitt, buzz

Category Challenge #2 (Page 52)

Possible answers include:
1. sips, stress, Seuss spins, sits, says, sis, sticks, skates
2. toot, trot, thought, test, treat, taught, tot, tart, tempt, tight
3. roar, rider, reindeer, racer, radar, radiator, rancher, ranger, regular, repair, ruler, rubber
4. Amanda, area, Arizona, aroma, aloha, antenna, aqua, Australia
5. dead, did, dad, dread, defend, demand, depend, divided, dud
6. noon, nun, notion, noun, napkin, nation, neon, nylon

Day After Day (Page 53)

1. Friday
2. Monday
3. 18th
4. Tuesday
5. 18th
6. Friday
7. Friday

What's Next? #1 (Page 54)

What's Next? #2 (Page 55)

Which Floor? (Page 56)

Neha: 5th floor   Will: 3rd floor
Sarah: 2nd floor   Katy: 1st floor
Brodie: 4th floor

Strain Your Brain (Page 57)

Possible answers include:

Things with holes: buttons, straws, strainers, scissors, needles, bagels

Things that are hot: sun, pepper, stove that's turned on, boiling water

Things that are green: broccoli, lettuce, celery, grass, leaves, asparagus, turtle

Things that you can wear on your feet: slippers, sandals, fins, boots, high heels, socks, sneakers

Animal Ad-VENN-tures (Page 58)

Possible answers include:
1. frog, salamander, rhinoceros
2. chipmunk, pony, leopard
3. porpoise, robin, chicken
4. iguana, coyote, ocelot
5. monkey, badger, beaver, gopher, weasel
6. pigeon, python, toucan
7. canary, bonito

More Ad-VENN-tures (Page 59)

Possible answers include:
1. respond, pinto, reply, terror, finish
2. inside, speeches, action, eager, thirteen
3. niece, fierce, patriot, limited
4. onto, into, ally, tidy, Tony
5. Maui
6. Oahu, Ohio, Iowa, aide
7. lose, most, best, cast, mint

Geometry Puzzle (Page 60)

1. N, F
2. Q
3. R
4. X
5. A, W
6. B, I
7. C, E
8. J, D

Volunteer Jobs (Page 61)

Curtis   sweeping sidewalks
Linda   selling snacks
Lin   selling tickets
Yonni   feeding animals
Collin   cleaning cages

Animal Scramble (Page 62)

1. bear
2. toad
3. camel
4. tiger
5. shark
6. spider
7. horse
8. leopard
9. zebra
10. llama
11. hamster
12. mouse
13. lion
14. beaver
15. snake

Odd Word Out (Page 63)

1. time (not a number)
2. blew (not a color)
3. tree (not a flower)
4. broccoli (not a fruit)
5. foot (not part of a face)
6. salmon (not a bird)
7. vase (not a geometric shape)
8. jacket (not something worn on the foot)
9. dresser (not something to sit on)
10. lizard (not an insect)
11. toward (not an adjective)
12. desk (not a verb)

Identify the Shapes (Page 64)

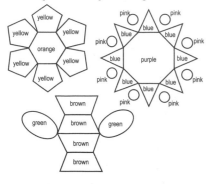

Solve the Riddle (Page 65)
You plug its nose with a clothespin.

Graph a Giraffe (Pages 66–67)

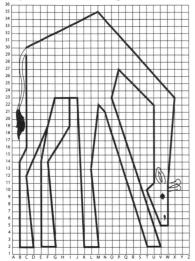

Color the Train (Page 68)

15	1	3	17	25	41	9	13	23	47	69
47	27	89	11	19	39	77	37	61	11	29
63	5	21	7	91	83	35	91	75	53	29
73	57	8	16	22	48	77	10	54	20	86
85	71	43	18	60	87	91	22	93	24	94
99	3	33	26	32	5	37	80	9	32	13
25	47	34	36	42	40	84	76	46	98	21
23	52	68	54	56	50	32	64	86	66	45
31	27	52	70	74	58	36	24	68	44	21
37	86	90	88	84	46	96	38	88	98	11
14	8	12	26	40	4	20	6	18	46	33
59	61	63	66	42	73	85	22	52	75	53
8	591	83	25	71	25	49	65	3	81	13
9	23	11	45	95	47	31	61	35	11	3
47	33	89	53	21	93	41	85	97	91	51
31	43	55	7	33	5	51	15	71	21	87

Riddle Time #1 (Page 69)
I dig you.

Riddle Time #2 (Page 70)
She got the point.

Cinquain Poem (Page 71)
Poems will vary.

Diamonte Poem (Page 72)
Poems will vary.

What's My Name? (Page 73)
Ferdinand Magellan

Draw a Monkey (Page 74)
Drawing will vary. Check for accuracy.

Draw a Fire Engine (Page 75)
Drawing will vary. Check for accuracy.

Best in Show (Pages 76–77)
The dog the judges picked for Best in Show was the chihuahua.

Repeated Patterns (Page 78)

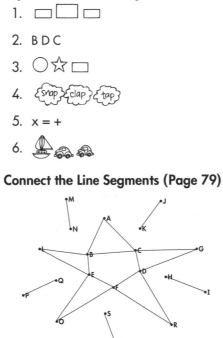

1. ▭ ▭ ▭
2. B D C
3. ○ ☆ ▭
4. snap clap tap
5. x = +
6. ⛵ 🚗 🚗

Connect the Line Segments (Page 79)

A star

Dot-to-Dot Vehicle (Page 80)
The vehicle is a tractor.

Cat and Mouse Dialogue (Page 81)
Answers will vary.

Between Friends Dialogue (Page 82)
Answers will vary.

Help the Dog Maze (Page 83)

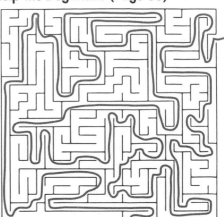

Help the Ant Maze (Page 84)

Crack the Code #1 (Page 85)
Riddle 1: Why are you always picking on me?
Riddle 2: He wanted a hot rod.

Crack the Code #2 (Page 86)
Riddle 1: Fifty pairs of pants.
Riddle 2: He had bat breath.

Crack the Code #3 (Page 87)
Riddle 1: He wanted to be in high school.
Riddle 2: In a top hat.

Complete the Teddy Bear (Page 88)
Drawing should be symmetrical.

Complete the House (Page 89)
Drawing should be symmetrical.

Complete the Zoo Entrance (Page 90)
Drawing should be symmetrical.

Complete the King (Page 91)
Drawing should be symmetrical.